Geoff Wilson was educated at King Henry VIII School, Coventry, and later graduated in civil engineering from Nottingham University. He subsequently obtained a postgraduate diploma from Imperial College, London. For a number of years, he was the Chief Civil Engineer employed by the largest multi-discipline architectural practice in Europe. Following this, he set up and controlled a steelwork fabricating company whilst acting as a private consulting engineer.

The major lesson learned during this period was that problems and their solutions often arise from the most unexpected quarters; a useful lesson which was applied throughout the search for the evidence concerning Robin Hood.

To my mother, whose leitmotif during my childhood was:

'If you don't know, look it up.'

Geoff Wilson

ROBIN HOOD – THE TRUTH BEHIND THE LEGEND

AUSTIN MACAULEY PUBLISHERS™

LONDON * CAMBRIDGE * NEW YORK * SHARJAH

Copyright © Geoff Wilson 2023

The right of Geoff Wilson to be identified as author of this work has been asserted by the author in accordance with sections 77 and 78 of the Copyright, Designs and Patents Act 1988.

All rights reserved. No part of this publication may be reproduced, stored in a retrieval system, or transmitted in any form or by any means, electronic, mechanical, photocopying, recording, or otherwise, without the prior permission of the publishers.

The story, the experiences, and the words are the author's alone.

A CIP catalogue record for this title is available from the British Library.

ISBN 9781035816880 (Paperback)
ISBN 9781035816897 (Hardback)
ISBN 9781035816903 (ePub e-book)

www.austinmacauley.com

First Published 2023
Austin Macauley Publishers Ltd®
1 Canada Square
Canary Wharf
London
E14 5AA

Because this book generally follows a completely different course from that of most of the other books on Robin and is based on completely different evidence, the research was carried out mainly by myself. However, there are a number of individuals who assisted in other ways. In particular, I would mention Ed Fenton, whose advice and encouragement, whilst not applying to what may be described as the technical content of the book, persuaded me to make major changes to the overall shape of the account, thereby rendering it much more readable and different from all the other books about Robin.

Also, my partner, Shirley, for organising photographic expeditions to the far corners of Yorkshire and for the time spent reading the draft documents to locate misspellings, mispunctuations, repetitions, omissions and all the other ambushes awaiting the unwary author; and Marjorie and Roger Horrell for investigating the local history of Bedale.

Table of Contents

Preface	11
Chapter 1: The Quest	13
Chapter 2: Landscape	19
Chapter 3: Medieval History	30
Chapter 4: Maps and Routes	41
Chapter 5: The Ballads	49
Chapter 6: Location	74
Chapter 7: The Religious Outlaw	95
Illustrations List of Maps	176
Details of Maps	177
List of Photographs	179
Details of Photographs	180

Preface

One of my early memories is being taken by my mother to see the film *The Adventures of Robin Hood*, starring Errol Flynn. Subsequently, I was given a copy of the book of the film and some of the images in the book are still clear in my mind many years later. For more than half of my life, I have lived within three and a half miles of Wentbridge in West Yorkshire, one of Robin's supposed locations. These events have firmly embedded an indelible interest in my mind. As a result I read any material I can find on Robin Hood, and have come to the conclusion that this material falls into three main categories. The first category is that which consists of serious commentaries on the various historical documents and actions. The second category includes the articles which blatantly promote the tourist attractions of a particular locality, and the third are those which merely deal with a Robin Hood type character but bear no resemblance to the real life and times of the outlaw.

In producing this study, I have made free use of many of these documents. In most cases, not as direct quotations or references but more as scraps of memories and ideas. In that sense, I have "stood on the shoulders of giants". I have drawn in particular on J C Holt's *Robin Hood*[1]. Whereas Holt has considered the complete repertoire of poems, plays and legends, I have concentrated mainly on the ballad *The Lytell Gest of Robin Hood*, which in view of my local knowledge, I consider to be an accurate record of the various locations described and therefore the most likely of the various ballads to be a true account of a real person.

History was never a particularly strong subject in my education, as is witnessed by the result of the last history examination I took at school when I achieved the remarkable feat of attaining sixty-eighth position out of a class of sixty-eight pupils with a mark of 12%. It takes a lot of effort and concentration to get a mark as low as that. In producing this present study, I have relied heavily on *A History of Britain* by Simon Schama[2] and *The Story of Britain* by Roy

Strong[3]. An unexpected outcome of this expedition into our history is the discovery that it is extremely interesting, and not the boring subject I had always believed it to be.

Finally, my knowledge of maps, roads and geology is derived from many years' experience as a civil engineer, enhanced by frequent references to *Britain's Structure and Scenery* by L Dudley Stamp[4].

1. J C Holt, *Robin Hood* Thames and Hudson (2011)
2. Simon Schama, A *History of Britain,* BBC Worldwide Ltd. (2000)
3. Roy Strong, *The Story of Britain,* Hutchinson (1996)
4. L Dudley Stamp, *Britain's Structure and Scenery*, Collins (1946)

Chapter 1
The Quest

*This is a story of long ago
At that time, the languages and letters were quite
different from ours of today.*

J R R Tolkien, *The Hobbit*

I had been working as a civil and structural engineer for nearly fifty years and had decided it was time to slow down and work part time from home. The children had moved out to make their own way in the world, so we had a couple of empty bedrooms one of which made an ideal office with a wide view over Barnsdale. As the seasons passed the field behind the house changed colour from white (winters were colder then) through varying shades of brown and green to the garish yellow of the oil seed rape or the softer gold of the ripened barley. For no reason other than curiosity, I investigated the origins of the word "barley" and found the Old English form was *beren*, which also meant the barn where barley was stored.

Three miles away, beyond the field, were the thickly wooded Went Hills intersected by possibly the southernmost, smallest and most attractive of the Yorkshire Dales; the valley of the River Went. With beren, a dale and trees in our vocabulary all that is required to make up the third stanza of the *Lytell Gest of Robyn Hood* is Robyn himself.

*Robyn stode in Bernesdale,
And lenyd hym to a tre;
And bi hym stode Litell Johnn
A gode yeman was he.*

> Robin stood in Barnsdale
> And leaned against a tree,
> And by him stood Little John
> A good yeoman was he

This raises the question, 'Was there a real Robyn Hood?' There is plenty of evidence but there is no proof and probably never will be. It is up to each individual to examine whatever evidence there is and draw their own conclusion. This book presents some of the evidence, most of it for the first time, and relates the story of the search for Robyn.

Innumerable books and articles have been produced about the legendary outlaw of Sherwood Forest, which fact prompts the question, why another one? What is different about this one? The answer is that this account tries to remove the story from the shadowy environs of museum archives or commercial websites, and relocate it in the real and harsh world of medieval England. It paints a picture on a broad canvass, of life and conditions at the time, drawing on inspiration from many sources including geology, topography and recorded history, as well as documents of various dates and degrees of reliability. When considering reports of historical events, if two events are claimed to have occurred at the same time, and in the same location it could be considered to be a coincidence. If more than two events are concurrent, it is less likely to be a coincidence. In fact, the more events which concur or are mutually supportive, the more likely it is that the relationship between them is causal rather than coincidental.

In 1982, Sir J C Holt, the eminent historian, produced his book *Robin Hood* which has become the standard reference work for almost all later writers and commentators on the subject. There have been two subsequent editions in 1989 and 2011. In addition, in 2010 the Folio Society issued a reprint of the 1989 edition.

In his prologue, Sir James wrote of Robin[1]:*He cannot be identified. There is a quiverful of possible Robin Hoods. Even the likeliest is little better than a shot in the gloaming. To substantiate an identity, the earliest tales of Robin's doings have to be matched with information from other sources. This is scanty. Moreover, even in the earliest stories there is no sure way of sifting fact from fiction. Hence who he might have been is inseparable from what he was thought to have been: any search for a man involves an analysis of the legend.*

The purpose of this book is to search for some of the "other sources" for the "scanty" information referred to by Holt. He refers to a "quiverful of possible Robin Hoods". In fact, there are an almost infinite number of Robin Hoods manufactured by an almost equal number of creators: writers from the fourteenth century to the present day; film producers from Hollywood and elsewhere; cartoon artists and almost anyone who felt inclined to comment. The character himself came in a number of guises: the leader of a gang of footpads or highway robbers; a poacher of the king's deer; a champion of the peasants who made up over 90% of the population; a robber of the rich who gave to the poor; and who apparently lived for almost 150 years spanning the reigns of six English kings, during which time he fought a ceaseless campaign against the Sheriff of Nottingham.

At a more basic level, there were two Robin Hoods. The best known is the fictitious, imaginary Robin Hood described above. The lesser known Robin is the real-life archetype, whose very existence is denied by many. It is the intention of this book to describe the life of this real person and to dispel some of the many myths attached to him through the fiction.

This book attempts to sort some of the fact from the fiction and draws on much of the information from the other sources briefly referred to by Holt. Among these other scanty sources is the author's personal knowledge of the physical characteristics of Sherwood Forest and Barnsdale, garnered from dwelling for over forty years in Nottingham and Barnsdale. Useful information was also gathered from maps, both modern and medieval. These included the Paris Map[2], The Gough Map[3], the later Ogilby maps[4], Jeffery's Map of Yorkshire[5] as well as more recent Ordnance Survey maps. Further information but on a much more modest scale was obtained from aerial photography.

Although Robin is very well known throughout the world, it is true that he cannot be identified as a person, but a lot of information about him can be collected if the various sources are diligently examined. His story is contained in a number of medieval ballads which were presented orally by minstrels, some of whom were servants of households, whilst others wandered from location to location, often stopping and performing at festivals, fairs and markets. Although many minstrels were servants attached to specific households, they often travelled to, and performed at other, usually local, establishments.[6]

The earlier minstrels generally presented ballads about distant and foreign places or historical events, real or fictitious, but later towards the end of the fourteenth and into the fifteenth century the courts and nobility became more sophisticated and their tastes changed. The role of the minstrels changed accordingly, they became known as troubadours, and the theme of their ballads became more romantic. Instead of tales of fights and trickery they tended to become more imaginary and included love stories.

Initially the ballads were presented orally, but later they were written in manuscript and later still, around 1500 and later, some were printed. In many cases, the copies which are currently available have parts missing or are damaged and there are also several copies of the same ballad which contain differing descriptions of the same events.

It is accepted that from time to time Robin acted as a footpad or highway robber. A prerequisite for following such a calling is a highway, so a considerable amount of attention has been given to investigating the form and layout of various medieval routes.

Inevitably, it has been necessary to cast doubts on previously produced claims. The names "Robin" or "Robert Hode" were, and are, relatively common English names. The fact that they are included in any documents, however authentic the document, is no evidence that they refer to any one particular individual, much less the legendary footpad. For example, the inclusion of no less than four Robert Hoods in the 2014 electoral roll for West Yorkshire is no evidence that the medieval outlaw is currently alive and well. Other commentators refer to places or features bearing the name Robin Hood. This approach is completely pointless as clearly demonstrated by Robin Hood Airport, located near Doncaster. Although it is reasonable to take due cognisance of place and feature names which have been in use for many years, particularly those of medieval origin.

It seems a number of historians and archivists have invested time and effort in trying to identify Robin as a known historical person. They have referred to court records and other official documents quoting a number of references to people, some with similar names and others whose names are completely different, but all are spread over a period of many years and counties. Typical of these individuals is Roger Godberd who is extensively referred to by Holt[7], Baldwin[8] and Bellamy[9]. These writers relate Godberd to the moated manor houses at Fenwick and Wellow, which they claim could be the castle described in the *Gest* as being within the wood, which they clearly believe refers to

Sherwood. They then proceed to admit that neither of these locations are actually within Sherwood Forest.

In view of the morass of information, much of it mutually contradictory, it was decided to apply the philosophy of Ockham's Razor and rely on the very basic information contained in the *Gest,* supplemented as little as possible with reference to selected historical documents. This information is augmented and confirmed by a study of undeniable data from other, apparently unconnected, sources. It is significant that all the attempts to identify Robin as a known historical person ignore his description in the *Gest,* as an unknown yeoman living in the greenwood. Rather than trying to deal with an unspecified number of candidates, I have selected and concentrated on this particular person.

As described above, the story is based on the ballads often presented orally by travelling minstrels as both entertainment and news bulletins, and in order to earn a livelihood. They would of course be in competition with other minstrels and in order to increase the appeal of their act would no doubt have introduced local references, depending on where they were performing at any particular time, much as characters in modern pantomimes and stand-up comedians do today. They will certainly have also introduced fictional episodes to amuse and even titillate their audience.

Most of the later ballads have been ignored, the only ones which have been taken into account here are the older ones, *A Lytell Gest of Robin Hood, Robin Hood and the Monk, Robin Hood and the Potter,* and *Robin Hood and Little John.* Of these the *Gest* has been analysed in considerable detail whereas the other three are considered only briefly.

It was decided to concentrate on the *Gest* not only because it is one of the earliest, but also because the descriptions it contains are more credible and the language used is more precise. Furthermore, the topography of the Barnsdale locality as described in the *Gest* is so accurate it cannot refer to any other locality. Having taken such care with this aspect of the story it is likely that the author or authors will not have strayed far from the truth in the remainder of the ballad. It is accepted in most of the versions of the story that Robin was a footpad or highway robber. It is essential therefore that a highway was located in his immediate locality. The accounts of the various travellers who were waylaid by Robin make it clear that this highway must be the main road from York to London. For this reason, the history and description of medieval roads in general, and of the Great North Road in particular, are dealt with at length and in some detail.

It has been shown using historical, topographical and cartographic evidence that many of the statements Holt has made, together with a number of the accepted "truths" about Robin Hood are incorrect, or at least doubtful. Some of the well-known facts which it is claimed are wrong include almost any in connection with Sherwood Forest, any connection with Lancashire and, unfortunately any connection with Maid Marian.

As far as I am aware no other writer has considered this approach and no one else appears to have even noticed the two great catastrophes which occurred at this time: the Great Famine which resulted in the deaths from malnutrition and starvation of ten percent of the population of England, and the Black Death which killed thirty percent of the remainder. It seems much more likely that Robin Hood died as a result of the plague than at the hands of a fornicating prioress.

1. C J Holt, *Robin Hood,* Thames & Hudson Ltd. (2011) p3
2. *The Paris Map,* British Library Board, (c1250)
3. *The Gough Map,* Bodleian Library, Oxford, (c1360)
4. *Ogilby maps,* (c1690)
5. *Jeffery's Map of Yorkshire,* (1771)
6. C J Holt, *Op. Cit.,* p.128
7. C J Holt, *Ibid.,* p.91–94, 189
8. D Baldwin, *Robin Hood,* Amberley Publishing Plc.,
9. J G Bellamy, *Robin Hood an historical enquiry* Indiana University Press, (1985) p33–34

Chapter 2
Landscape

The story of Robin Hood begins during the geological Carboniferous epoch about 350 million years ago, when a great thickness of sandstone, clays, limestones and the coal measures were being laid down in the area which is now northern England. Subsequently during the Permian epoch a layer of calciferous sludge was being superimposed on the carboniferous rocks. After 250 million years of being compressed, folded, eroded and subjected to chemical change, it formed a stratum of Magnesian Limestone. A hundred million years later during the Jurassic epoch a similar layer of calciferous sludge was deposited in the same area. This resulted in a stratum of limestone known as the Jurassic Oolite at a higher level than the Magnesian Limestone.

These rocks were subsequently subjected to tectonic compression in a mainly east-west direction which resulted in the formation of the Pennines, the so-called backbone of England. The Pennines in their turn cause problems with travel from east to west in northern and central England.

Trans-Pennine travel is assisted by three gaps in the range of hills, the Tyne gap in the north, and then the Stainmore gap and finally the Aire gap in the south. The Stainmore gap reaches a height of 1380 feet above sea level and as a result is less significant as a trans-pennine route than the other two, particularly in winter. The Aire gap is formed by the rivers Humber, Aire and Ribble and it is the Aire gap which is of particular interest and importance to the Robin Hood story.

Because limestone is generally more resistant to erosion than the underlying rocks, the Magnesian and Oolitic limestones form two parallel ranges of low hills. Although only slightly higher than the surrounding land surface, these hills, like the rivers, are of great significance to the story.

The River Calder flows from west to east and joins the River Aire near the present location of Castleford; they then join the River Humber before flowing into the North Sea. During the Ice Age which lasted many thousands of years most of Britain north of the line joining the River Severn and the Wash was buried beneath a great thickness of ice, which was not stationary but was moving slowly southwards and westwards. As it moved it scraped and gouged rock detritus from the base rocks beneath it, transported it many miles, and finally deposited it in a completely new location. This material and the material resulting from the weathering of the varying bedrocks formed the disparate soils presently covering many parts of England and as a result, the flora and fauna similarly varied from location to location.

At one stage, the mouth of the River Humber was blocked by ice and a lake, sometimes referred to by geologists as Lake Humber, formed extending from near York in the north to Grantham in the south, and with an arm filling the Aire valley as far as Leeds[1]. As the ice melted at the end of the Ice Age, some 10,000 years ago, the lake waters were released and the bed of the lake became a low-lying marshy area. Further melting of the ice, with a subsequent increase in sea levels, resulted in the formation of the English Channel and the final separation of England from the European land mass, and therefore creating the political situation existing at the time of Robin Hood.

As the climate became warmer and the ice sheets melted, the land surface became covered in hardy trees and bushes which then gave way to dense deciduous woodland generally known as the Wildwood. The first inhabitants of the country were hunter gatherers. They later cleared some areas of woodland to enable them to grow crops, rather than having to gather wild plants and fruit and they kept animals. They also required wood for building and for fuel, so more areas of the Wildwood were cleared of trees and bushes. In other areas, the soil was not suitable for supporting woodland, and the land surface became covered with grassland, heath or moors. Farming and the domestication of animals removed the necessity of hunting wild animals for food, but it continued as a sport or pastime.

Roads, tracks and foot-ways are also important features of a local landscape. The early hunter gatherers would no doubt have settled in locations which were easily defend-able and sheltered from the weather. The need for cooperation in defence and hunting large game resulted in the growth of settlements and villages. They would also have located sources of food, water and the haunts of animals which would probably not have been adjacent to the settlements, thereby necessitated travelling, initially by foot. The regular use of these routes would have led to the formation of trails which in many cases would require in places, the clearing of bushes undergrowth and trees.

As some people took to travelling on horseback, it would also have required the clearance of plant and tree branches overhead. Later as carts and wagons came into use the width of the tracks also had to be increased.

After their conquest of Britain and in order to more easily control the Britons, the Romans built many roads. At the time, many lowland areas were un-drained and liable to flooding. To avoid these areas the Romans tended to site the roads on the higher ground. In general, therefore, the road currently known as Ermine Street, the main route from London and the South to York and the North ran along the crest of the limestone ridge.

The River Aire, however, presented a problem. Where it cuts through the ridge the river is narrower but deeper than to the east or west. The Romans probably found the river too deep to ford at this point but were able to locate two sites where the river could be forded. One was at Castleford and the second forty miles further east across the River Humber. The estuary of the Humber is funnel-shaped which affects the tides and in fact two of the tributaries of the Humber, the Trent and the Ouse, are both affected by tidal bores known locally as eigers. Whilst the Humber itself is not affected by the Eigers it is clear that the tide at the crossing point would rise fairly rapidly and the range would be rather more than at the actual coast. At the crossing point, near the present Humber Bridge, the river is one and a half miles wide and tidal. Crossing here would be difficult and unreliable especially during stormy weather.

The site near Castleford is not located where the river crosses the limestone ridge but five miles west at the site of the old glacial lake where it could be more easily forded. In fact, archaeologists have recently discovered the stone slabs laid by the Romans on the river bed to form the ford. To reach this point on the river, the road is diverted westwards at Barnsdale Bar which is about nine miles south of the river, and returns to the higher ground one mile north of the river. Although the river is fordable at this point, the land to the north of the river, the old lake bed, is low-lying and marshy. Crossing the river here would have still been difficult, especially when the marshes were flooded.

The Venerable Bede records that in 655 when the Mercians were fleeing after the Battle of Winwoed, probably using the old Roman road, more drowned in the marshes than were killed by the Northumbrians. Later in 1069, when William the Conqueror was leading his army north to put down a rebellion at York and to harry the North, he was delayed for three weeks as the river at Castleford was in flood and the marshes on the north bank were inundated.

In the early fourteenth century, the land enclosures, which caused problems and hardships for many of the peasants, were still some two or three centuries in the future. The typical English hedges, fences and ditches which later produced the well-known chequer board pattern of fields were non-existent. The majority of the land was uncultivated, and depending on the underlying soils, would have been largely moors, heath, woodland or common grazing land. Small villages would probably have had three or more large unfenced fields which would have been divided into a large number of narrow strips, owned or rented by individuals who paid for them by rendering homage, military service, and other services to the lord of the manor.

By claiming the rights granted to them by Magna Carta in 1215, the barons and landowners were able to force the king to disafforest large areas of Sherwood, so that by the beginning of the fourteenth century the forest occupied 172 square miles, as shown on the map 7. Although the boundaries of Sherwood Forest changed from time to time, at any particular time they were fixed by law and were recorded.

The boundaries of the area known as Barnsdale on the other hand, vary not only with time but also depending on the authority describing them. Holt and others claim that Barnsdale is an area centred on the valley of a small stream known as The Skell, which flows from west to east and is crossed by the Great North Road near Robin Hood's Well, close to the village of Skelbrooke, some five and a half miles north of Doncaster. Holt however admits in his book "Robin Hood" that his description of the topography of Barnsdale is based on the 1/25,000 and 6inch Ordnance Survey maps. The description of the topography given here is based on living for over forty years within three miles of Wentbridge and many hours walking in the area known as Barnsdale.

It is also claimed by some that Barnsdale is centred on the village of Hampole situated one mile south of Skelbrooke and four miles south of Wentbridge. These three traditional locations are so close it is irrelevant which is considered although Wentbridge is the only one mentioned in the *Gest* and the valley of the River Went is the only geophysical feature likely to have been considered when the name was adopted. .In view of the later suggestion of a connection with

Richard Rolle, the reference to Hampole by some early commentators may be very significant.

As described elsewhere, little or no importance is attached to names of places or localities incorporating Robin Hood's name. One exception however is Robin Hood's Stone. There is, in the archives of Monk Bretton Priory, a copy of a deed dated 1422 which defines the location of a plot of land by reference to the "Stone of Robin Hode" sited in the fields of "Sleep Hill".

Although the stone itself has not been located, the name "Sleep Hill" appears on the "one inch" and 1:25 000' Ordnance Survey maps produced since the first edition in 1840.

Also a lane currently named on the Ordnance Survey maps as "Sleep Hill Lane" runs from Wrangbrook to Skelbrooke and for its entire length it lies in the shallow valley of the Skell and at no point is it further than 200yds from the stream The lane is approximately one and a quarter miles in length and the maximum variation in level is no more than ten feet, so obviously Sleep Hill is not actually on the line of the lane. However, on the north east side of the lane the land rises 120 feet to form a low hill at the top of which is the road junction currently known as Barnsdale Bar. The One Inch Ordnance Survey map published in 1840 shows a toll gate on the turnpike road from Barnsdale to Leeds which was completed in 1822, but does not include the name Barnsdale Bar.

The latest 1/25,000 Ordnance Survey Explorer map shows the name "Sleep Hill" immediately adjacent to a bend in "Sleep Hill Lane". However, this is clearly a printing error as on all previous maps the note is "Sleep Hill Quarry" and is obviously seen on site to be a small abandoned quarry.

The reference to Robin Hood's name in a legal document and the connection with Barnsdale only seventy or so years after his supposed death is a clear indication that he was a real, living and well-known person and not some fictional creation, as is often claimed.

The 1840 Ordnance Survey map was published in four quarters with Barnsdale Bar lying almost on the intersection of the four sheets. On the north east section, there are some small fields shown adjacent to the main road whereas they are not shown on the south east section published a few weeks later. It may well be that these are the original fields of Sleep Hill adjacent to which stood Robin Hoods Stone.

On 16 April 1473, Sir John Paston wrote from Norfolk to his brother William and explained that his stable boy had gone to Bernysdale to take part in a play about *Seynt Jorge and Robyn Hode and the Shryff of Nottingham*. It seems likely that a number of people would also have been travelling to Barnsdale for the same reason. By 1473, going from Norfolk to Barnsdale would have involved travelling north from Doncaster to Barnsdale Bar on the old Roman road, but forking right onto the newer route through Wentbridge at Barnsdale Bar. It is possible, or even likely, that there would have been a stone way marker at the junction. It may have carried an inscription including the name "Robin Hood", or it may just have been known locally as "Robin Hood's Stone". In either case, it is clear that Robin Hood was well known at the time and was linked to Barnsdale. The precise location of the stone is not known at the present time, except that it was located in Sleep Hill Fields. Sleep Hill is north of the Skell where it is crossed by the Great North Road. It is conjectured that a logical location for the stone would be by the roadside at the fork where the newer road through Wentbridge leaves the old Ermine Street. This would have been some 350 yards south of the present road junction of the Great North Road, the A1 and Wrangbrook Lane.

It is recorded that after he was crowned in 1485 King Henry VII left Doncaster and travelled north. He was met by the Earl of Northumberland with a large group of people at Barnsdale, *a litill beyonde Robyn Haddez-ston,* (Robin Hood's Stone). It is clear from this statement that the stone was close to the road and north of the Skell and it is unlikely therefore that Barnsdale is centred on the Skell but much more likely to be centred on the valley of the River Went. If the king proceeded beyond the stone for about half a mile, he would have arrived at Barnsdale Bar just two and a half miles from Wentbridge.

On the Ordnance Survey sheets 278 and 279 of the Explorer series, the river Skell is not dignified with the title "River" Skell but is merely described as The Skell. In fact, unlike other neighbouring streams, it is not named at all on the 1840 Ordnance Survey maps although the villages of Skellow and Skelbrooke are.

The original source of the Skell is difficult to locate using current maps. It is shown in different positions on the Google maps and on the Ordnance Survey maps. However on the 1771 Jeffery's Map (map 3) it is clearly shown at the west end of the village of Upton from where the stream flows eastwards to Wrangbrook. During the middle of the twentieth century Upton colliery was constructed some two and a half miles south of Wentbridge. The colliery site is on the southern flank of Upton beacon, a limestone outlier, and is the location of several springs. During the commissioning and closure of the colliery there were extensive engineering works which would have inevitably changed the layout of the surface drainage.

The stream then flows as a minor brook for three and three quarters of a mile before joining Hampole Dike to form the Old Ea Beck which is in turn a tributary of the River Don. The valley of the Skell is insignificant as shown by the wide spacing of the contours on the map, despite the fact that they are at a vertical interval of only 15 feet. The land surface on the south west side of the stream can best be described as undulating and can hardly be considered as forming a dale. The stream itself at its widest part is only six or eight feet wide and only a few inches deep.

The river Went, on the other hand, rises near Featherstone and flows some twenty miles in an easterly direction to join the River Don near Thorne. The valley of the river is completely different from that of the Skell.

Although it is only two miles downstream from Wentbridge to Kirk Smeaton the Went Valley, which is probably the most southerly of the Yorkshire dales, is considered in three sections known as Wentdale, Brockadale and Smeaton Pastures. The central part known as Brockadale is currently a nature reserve. The origin of the name "Brockadale" is not clear but it may have originally been Brocket Dale or the valley of the young red deer, or the name may have referred to the rocky or broken valley sides.

Brockadale has been described by the Yorkshire Wildlife Trust [2] as a craggy, steep-sided gorge formed after the last ice-age when glacial melt-water, no doubt flowing from Lake Humber described above, burst through the Magnesian limestone rock. In places such as Smeaton Crags and Long Crag, the valley sides consist of exposed sheer rock surfaces. In general, the valley sides are so steep that they have never been cultivated and the vegetation consists mainly of thick ancient woodland, the trees themselves are probably descendants of the trees present at the time of Robin Hood. One particularly important topographical feature is a hill known as Sayles or Salis which forms part of the southern side of the Went Valley, and plays a significant part in the Robin Hood story. Very close to Sayles is Castle Hill which is a rocky bluff overlooking the valley and was the site of an Iron Age settlement. In the more recent past, many iron-age settlements were described as forts, although this was not necessarily their main function. It is believed the name "Castle Hill" arose as a result of this misconception. Unfortunately, the evidence of the existence of the fort or enclosure was destroyed by more recent quarrying activities in the nineteenth century. Presumably this location would have been chosen as it was a good defensive position. A factor which Robin might well have considered when choosing his retreat.

For convenience, this whole two-mile stretch of the Went Valley from Wentbridge to Kirk Smeaton will be referred to here as Wentdale.

Holt claims [3], without producing any evidence, that the totally insignificant valley of the Skell is the true centre of Barnsdale but ignores the quite dramatic Went valley only three miles north. Jeffery's Map of 1771 and the 1840 one-inch Ordnance Survey map both place the name "Barnsdale" almost exactly midway between the Skell and Wentdale, at the location of the present Barnsdale Bar service station on the Great North Road. The marked difference between Wentdale and the valley of the Skell is clearly illustrated in the photographs and the cross-sections (map 10). Wentdale is such an outstanding topographical feature that it would certainly have been well known locally and possibly even further afield. It is clear that the area known as Barnsdale can only be centred on Wentdale. Despite extensive searches of maps and literature, it has proved impossible to find any reference to a named dale in connection with The Skell.

The northern boundary of Barnsdale was possibly defined by John Leland, antiquary to King Henry VIII, in the early sixteenth century when he recorded that he had observed:

Along on the lift hond, a iii miles of betwixt Milburne and Feribridge…the wooddi and famose forest of Barnesdale, wher they say Robyn Hudde lyvid like an owtlaw.

Currently, there is no Milburne but if it is assumed the reference is to Milford this appears to indicate that Barnsdale extended as far north as the River Aire, and if this is the case, possibly as far south as the River Don. It has also been suggested that Barnsdale extends from Badsworth in the west to Askern in the east which means the total area would be about eight miles by 15 miles.

Immediately upstream from Wentbridge there is an area of low-lying marsh known as "Thorp Marsh". In the medieval period, the river in this area was undefined, but a short length through the marsh was straightened probably in the early eighteenth century. It has been claimed that the work was carried out by Cornelius Vermuyden the Dutch engineer but this is not a tenable claim as

Vermuyden died in 1677 and the original course of the river is shown on Jefferey's map produced a century later. Jefferey's map also shows the river following a different course downstream of Wentbridge so it is clear that it could have occupied any position across the flat valley bottom during the seven hundred or so years we are considering here.

As mentioned above the first reference to Barnsdale in the *Gest* is as early as the third Stanza:

Robyn stode in Bernesdale,
And lenyd hym to a tre;
And bi hym stode Litell Johnn
A gode yeman was he.

Robin stood in Barnsdale,
And leaned against a tree
And by him stood Little John
A good yeoman was he.

Holt and others claim that the name Barnsdale originates from Beorn's valley, but give no indication of who "Beorn" was or his connection with the location. Perhaps this was just a guess or assumption.[3] Reference to the Old English Translator on the internet shows that the Old English word "beorn" translates as a "chief" or "strong man" rather than a personal name whereas "beren" was the origin of the modern word "barley" and hence "barn" as a place where barley was stored. The name "Barnsdale" is probably just what it says, the valley or area where barley is cultivated or the valley with a barn. Barley prospers better than other cereal crops on alkaline soils which are derived from the weathering of the limestone in the area. It is also noted from personal observation that barley is still (2014) a major cereal crop in the area. Although the sides of the Went valley were not cultivated, there is geophysical and aerial photographic evidence of cultivation on the dip slope of the escarpment between the Went valley and Barnsdale Bar, although the physical evidence has since been destroyed by extensive quarrying operations.

Approximately eleven miles south-east of Wentbridge is the town of Barnsley which was first mentioned in the Domesday Book in 1089. The local authority's website suggests the name originates from the old English word beren, which is shown above to be related to a barn or to barley, combined with lee or ley an uncultivated field or land. It is quite possible that due to the proximity of Barnsley and Wentbridge and the similarity between their names that the area known as Barnsdale extended eastwards as far as Barnsley.

When considering the actions and lifestyle of a highway robber or footpad, the appearance of roads in the medieval landscape is quite significant. It appears that there were virtually no restrictions on where the traveller could go. It was quite common for individuals on approaching a particular area, which was too soft or muddy or on the other hand possibly too stony and rough, to follow an adjacent alternative course. This often had the effect of creating a series of parallel tracks, so effectively the road became many feet wide. The traveller virtually had the right to go where he wanted, even if this meant trampling on and destroying crops.

The first legislation affecting roads in England was probably the Statute of Winchester passed in 1285 by King Edward I which stated:...*that the highways from market towns to other market towns be widened where there are woods or hedges or ditches, so that there may be no ditch, underwood or bushes where one could hide with evil intent within two hundred feet of the road on one side or the other...*

Apart from this requirement there was no stipulation as to the width of any road, so where the surface became rocky or muddy, travellers would seek out the easiest route, and the road therefore gradually increased in width. In some translations of stanza 21 of the *Gest,* the knight is described as following a secret track. As he was travelling over a very difficult part of his route on the steep valley side at Wentbridge, it may well be there were a number of multiple tracks, and if the area was wooded, as it probably was, and as it still is, the track he was following would almost certainly have been well hidden from any observers.

It appears that no one was responsible for the upkeep or maintenance of the roads and tracks. As a route approached a local restriction, say a bridge or ford, the various tracks would merge into one, resulting in an increase in the traffic intensity and a consequent deterioration in the condition of the road. In such localities, the local populace, often under the direction of the church would undertake some maintenance work. Payment would be made by absolution of sins or a reduction in the tithes being claimed. Bridges would be constructed under the direction of the clergy and the bridges often included a chantry chapel, where travellers could pray and make a votive offering or pay a toll to pay for future maintenance.

1. L D Stamp, *Britain's Structure and Scenery* Collins (1948) p166
2. Yorkshire Wildlife Trust *Brockadale Nature Reserve* Internet.
3. C J Holt, *Robin Hood* Thames and Hudson (2011) p 86]

Chapter 3
Medieval History

In dealing with any historic occurrence establishing the period to be considered is of prime importance, as this then limits the documents and events which should be investigated. It is generally accepted that in 1377 a writer named William Langland wrote an allegorical narrative poem entitled "Piers Plowman". In the poem, one character named Friar Sloth says, 'I do not know my paternoster perfectly as the priest sings it. But I do know the rhymes of Robin Hood and Ranulf Earl of Chester.' This clearly indicates that Robin Hood lived and was well known before 1377.

In the *Gest,* there is a reference to "Edwarde our comly kynge". Some commentators have suggested that this may refer to Edward the Confessor, who died in 1066. However, there are also many references to the Sheriff of Nottingham. There was no sheriff of Nottingham before 1377 but a "Sheriff of Nottinghamshire, Derbyshire and the Royal Forests" was appointed in 1068, two years after the death of Edward the Confessor. The title "Sheriff of Nottinghamshire, Derbyshire and the Royal Forests" is rather cumbersome so it would not be easy to incorporate it in a line of poetry. It is to be expected that it would be shortened to the "Sheriff of Nottingham" both in the poem and in everyday usage. The longer title also explains why the Sheriff of Nottingham had jurisdiction over Barnsdale Forest in Yorkshire, although the status of Barnsdale is not known. In many instances, it is referred to as "Barnsdale Forest" whereas elsewhere the term "Barnsdale" is used, possibly referring merely to an area or region...

Edward I became king in 1272 and Edward III died in 1377, so it is fairly certain that Robin Hood lived in the period between 1272 and 1377. This is the Robin and the period of time we will be investigating. Apart from the *Gest* there are two other early poems which fall within this period and are therefore significant. "Robin Hood and the Potter" and "Robin Hood and the Monk". Other tales and poems may have been added to the story much later. For example, it is understood that Maid Marian did not appear until the reign of Henry VIII some two hundred years later.

Having established the period during which Robin Hood lived, it is important to consider the conditions and way of life prevailing at the time. The Norse settlements in Iceland and Greenland during the ninth and tenth centuries are evidence that the climate in northern Europe was more benign than at present, and this of course had an effect in Britain as well. During the first three centuries following the Norman Conquest the population of England trebled to three million. Initially, because of the benign climate the food supply was sufficient to cope with the additional demand, apart from the occasional poor year. However towards the end of the thirteenth century the climate began to deteriorate and the population began to suffer from a certain amount of deprivation.

When Edward the Confessor died in January 1066, Harold Godwinesstone became king of England. There were however two other claimants to the English throne, Harald Hardrada, king of Norway, and William, Duke of Normandy. Harold was aware that Hardrada intended to launch an attack in the north of England and in order to avoid a winter campaign this attack would take place in the spring or summer. Harold prepared to repel this invasion by moving his troops and his fleet to York early in the year. The threatened attack did not materialise so, in the late summer, Harold dispersed his troops and withdrew his fleet to London.

In September, he received news that Hardrada had crossed the North Sea and had sailed up the River Ouse as far as Riccall, only ten miles from York. Gathering his troops with all their equipment and supplies Harold left London and marched the 200 miles to Stamford Bridge, about eight miles east of York in just five days. On 25 September, he took the Vikings by surprise and gained a decisive victory during which Hardrarda was killed.

Three days later, with Harold and his army still in the north, William of Normandy landed unopposed at Pevensey on the south coast. Harold was forced to repeat his march of a few days before, but in the opposite direction. His troops, no doubt exhausted by their journeying and having suffered losses at Stamford Bridge, were defeated at Hastings only three weeks after the earlier battle, and Harold himself was killed. This of course was the beginning of the period which became known as the Norman Conquest. At the time of the conquest, the Saxon population of England numbered about one million, so they greatly outnumbered the invading Normans and over a few generations they tended to absorb the Normans. Although Latin was still the preferred language for legal and ecclesiastical use, the French and Norman-French languages fell out of use, and English became the accepted language for everyday and literary use, although it did incorporate many French and Norman words and expressions.

After the English had been defeated and William had been crowned king of England, the Norman rule was particularly harsh. During the five or six years after the battle of Hastings the Saxons rebelled on many occasions and in many locations. In 1069, the Saxon English north of the River Humber rebelled, so William and his army travelled north. Because the swamps on the north bank of the river Aire were inundated, he was delayed for two or three weeks at Castleford near Pontefract but then moved on to York. They ransacked the town, plundered the monasteries and laid waste large areas of the surrounding countryside. Houses and cottages were burned, crops destroyed, farm implements were wrecked and animals slaughtered. The whole episode became known as the "Harrying of the North".

An important aspect of the conquest was the confiscation of the larger Saxon estates and their distribution by William among his allies and particularly those who had taken part in the invasion. The main innovation of this period was the introduction of the feudal system. Under this arrangement the land was considered as being the property of the king and the tenure thereof was granted to barons and bishops in return for rent or services. They in turn granted tenure to knights who in turn granted similar rights to the villeins. Rather than holding a single area of land each tenant would hold a number of divided and often quite widely separated honours, manors, and fiefs. Areas of land were then sublet to the villeins who were normally Saxon peasants who paid for them by rendering various services and other payments to their landlords. In many cases, the conditions imposed on the sub-tenants by their landlords were very harsh.

Many of the more recent stories of Robin Hood, in particular films and television programmes, depict him as fighting the Normans on behalf of his oppressed Saxon colleagues. It is believed that in fact Robin was not active until about three hundred years after the conquest, and that the problems at that time were due to natural events as well as the results of human and political activities.

Richard I came to the throne in 1189 and although he reigned for almost ten years, he was away from the country for most of that time. Part of this absence was due to the fact that on his return from the crusade he was shipwrecked, taken prisoner and held for ransom by the Duke of Austria and later by the Holy Roman Emperor. Meanwhile, the population was still increasing, the climate was deteriorating so crops were failing, and the money for the king's ransom had to be raised by taxation. The king died in 1199 and was succeeded by his younger brother John.

Among many unpopular measures John imposed, was forest law on large areas of the country, Sherwood Forest for example, covered almost the whole area of Nottinghamshire. He was also making constant demands for funds to finance his ongoing war with France. The barons began to become disturbed by the actions of the king and in 1215 eventually forced him to seal the Magna Carta. Despite the king's resistance, the barons forced him and his successor Henry III to adhere to the provisions of the charter and as a result of their new found power, they were able to reduce the amount of land subject to forest laws. A result of this was that by the time Robin Hood was active, the area of the forest had been reduced to that shown on map 7.

Henry died in 1272 and was succeeded by his eldest son Edward I, who reigned until his death in July 1307. In 1285, Edward sponsored the Statute of Winchester which contained the following provision:

It is likewise commanded that the highways from market towns to other market towns be widened where there are woods or hedges or ditches, so that there may be no ditch, underwood or bushes where one could hide with evil intent within two hundred feet of the road on one side or the other, provided that this statute extends not to oaks or to large trees so long as it is clear underneath.

It seems clear that highway robbery was quite common at the end of the thirteenth century.

In 1307, Edward I was succeeded by his son, also named Edward, who proved to be an ineffective and very unpopular monarch. He tended to ignore the barons and chose unpopular companions whose advice he relied on to the exclusion of others.

Edward II was unfortunate that the early part of his reign was affected by two major events beyond his control. He came to the throne in the midst of the Scottish war of Independence in which the Scots led by Robert the Bruce and William Wallace constantly carried out plundering raids on the north of England.

In fact, he was forced to fight four battles against the Scots in the first twelve months of his reign.

The second major event occurred in 1315. As described above there had been a gradual deterioration in the climate during the thirteenth century, and due to the increasing population, a series of shortages and minor famines were experienced. But in there was a sudden and dramatic change in the European climate. The area affected extended from Russia in the east to the Pyrenees Mountains in the west and included the whole area from Britain in the north to Italy in the south. The effect of the change was to greatly increase the rainfall and lower the temperatures. Due to the cold and water-logged soil, seed which had already been sown failed to germinate causing widespread crop failures. In addition of course, pasture and the natural vegetation which provided fodder for domestic animals and for wildlife was also affected.

People were forced to eat the seed which had been put aside for sowing the following spring. As their domestic animals died, they were forced to kill the farm and draught animals, and the people themselves became so weakened by malnutrition that their resistance to disease was also weakened. In general, life in the fourteenth century was physically very hard merely to survive, and as a result of the illnesses and lack of sustenance they had been physically weakened and so even after the climate returned to the normal pre-famine status, they were unable to put in the effort on the land necessary to restore their former standard of living. There were reports of parents abandoning their children, older people deliberately starving themselves so the younger generations might survive, and even in some cases people resorting to cannibalism. Despite the measures taken to preserve their lives, around ten percent of the population died as a result of starvation and malnutrition.

It has been suggested that the climate change resulted from the effects of the eruption of Mount Tarawera, a fissure volcano in New Zealand which violently erupted in about 1315. Some experts claim the eruption lasted for approximately two years until about 1317, but others reckon it may have lasted much longer, possibly until 1321–1322. It is believed the ash and dust cloud from the volcano affected the weather in Europe. After the eruption ceased, there was an almost coincident improvement in the European weather, but the effects of the famine lasted for several years, in fact according to some estimates until 1325/1326. This ten-year period became known as the Great Famine.

As a result of the gradual deterioration of the climate and the resulting crop failures and occasional famines in the thirteenth century, there was widespread hardship and a general increase in the cost of living. This led to a corresponding increase in crime and anti-social behaviour ranging from petty offences such as theft and poaching, to acts of physical violence. Despite the draconian punishments, even including execution, imposed on the perpetrators the number of crimes continued to increase. After the outbreak of the Great Famine in 1315, conditions became even worse and poaching of the royal deer increased, leading to increasing tensions between the king and the general population.

The manor rolls of Wakefield record that a certain Robert Hode appears in court in 1320 and several times shortly thereafter. He is given permission to build a five-roomed house near the market, but later he is accused of failing to report for military action against the Scots, breaking forest laws and resisting the lord of the manor. There is no clear evidence that this man is the Robin Hood we are interested in, or indeed if it is just one man or several having the same name.

At this time, Thomas the Earl of Lancaster called for men to join his rebellion against King Edward II. Robin Hode is not listed as failing to report for duty in the rebellion so it is assumed he was one of the rebels. On 16 March 1322, the earl was defeated at the Battle of Boroughbridge and taken to Pontefract Castle, where he was held prisoner and was beheaded on 22 March. The rebels were outlawed and the records in Wakefield show a five-roomed house near the market was confiscated; perhaps this was Robert Hode's house.

It has been suggested that Robin was outlawed for his part in the rebellion, but it is also possible that he chose of his own free will to take refuge in the forest to enable him to follow his own religious beliefs, without fear of being persecuted for heresy. Other rebels, named in the court records were John Nailer (Little John), W Schakelok (Will Scarlet) and Roger of Doncaster. Presumably they also were outlawed or fled with Robin to the forest. If Robin was in fact involved in the Battle of Boroughbridge in 1322 and died in 1349 as suggested below, it seems reasonable to assume he was born around the turn of the century, about 1300.

Despite the king's victory over the rebels at Boroughbridge, he still remained very unpopular and even despised by many of his subjects. He died, probably murdered, some five years later in 1327. His eldest son, although only nine years old, was crowned as his successor, Edward III. Because the new king was so young the country was ruled initially by his mother Isabella and her lover, Roger

Mortimer, the Earl of March. There was no improvement in the way the country was ruled and only three years later there was an uprising by the king, supported by better friends and advisers. Mortimer was tried and executed and the queen later became a nun. Unlike his father Edward III became a successful and popular king whose reign lasted for some 50 years.

In the fourteenth century, almost the entire population were peasants who lived in basic timber framed huts with wattle and daubed walls and thatched roofs, gathered together into small villages. In contrast, the village churches were usually well-built stone buildings with a tower or spire and glass windows. In the towns and cities, the great cathedrals dominated the towns. Typical examples were Salisbury and Lichfield. Although the construction was extended over many years, Salisbury was finally completed in 1258 and Lichfield in 1340.

Roman Catholicism was the only permitted religion and any deviation from the Church's teaching or practices was considered heretical. The organisation of the Church was very hierarchical with the village priest, who was often very poorly educated and poorly paid, at the lowest level of the clergy and the bishops and archbishops at the top with the pope at the summit.

The population in general, both peasants and townspeople, believed explicitly in the teachings of the church. To them God, Heaven, Hell and Purgatory were real and terrifying. They also believed God was omnipotent and was responsible for every occurrence that was not readily explained by their own every day experiences. They also believed that the king was chosen by God and ruled by divine right.

The Church did everything possible to foster these beliefs and fears and used them to effectively take control of everyone's daily life. The Church taught for example that a person who had not been baptised, was living with a partner without being married, did not pay their dues to the church or were not buried in consecrated ground would not be allowed to enter Heaven. The Churches demands were extremely onerous; not only were people forced to hand over one tenth of their income, whether that was in the form of money or produce, but they also had to work on church land without payment. This was particularly irksome for peasants during times of intense activity such as spring and harvest time, as they would also need to be putting in extra efforts at the same time to cultivate their own land to provide for their families.

Following the famine in the fourteenth century life expectancy at birth was about thirty years, but this was mainly due to the high rates of infant and childhood mortality. Those children who survived into their late teens could well expect to live into their fifties or sixties and even in some cases to their eighties. As a result of the large number of childhood deaths and the fact that most births and deaths occurred in the home these two occurrences became a common fact of everyday life, as did the accompanying rites of passage, the baptisms, confirmations and funerals, all of which generated income for the Church.

The permanent presence of death in their lives obviously led the general populace to turn their attention to the afterlife. The general belief was that after death the souls of the departed, even those who had apparently spent a blameless life would have been tainted by original sin. Everyone would therefore expect to spend some time after their death in purgatory, where they would have to atone for their sins, however insignificant, by pain and suffering before proceeding to heavenly bliss. Although, there was no support for the concept of purgatory in the bible or in the scriptures, it was fully supported by the Church. The interior of church walls was brightly painted with murals showing the saints and angels in heaven and also the torments of souls in purgatory. Later, during the reformation, these paintings were whitewashed or plastered over, but at the time they presented a very real reminder of what awaited everyone after death.

The length of time a soul spent in purgatory was determined by the extent or intensity of their sinning on earth, but this could be reduced by an individual obtaining indulgences for themselves by purchasing them from the Church before their death, or by their friends or relations after their death, arranging and paying for, masses to be said by the priest on their behalf. In addition of course, the Church had income from tithes and other businesses such as sheep farming, providing financial services and rent from church owned property. Some of the monasteries had rather surprising sources of income: rent from brothels and heavy industrial work for instance. There is perhaps surprisingly, evidence of the existence of a blast furnace for iron smelting at Rievaulx Abbey in North Yorkshire.

In contrast to the general population, the Church was in the privileged position of not having to pay taxes on its income, so over a period of time it accrued an immense amount of wealth as witnessed by the great medieval cathedrals and monasteries. From time to time, considerable amounts would be sent to the headquarters in Rome. The centre for collection in the north of England was of course York, from where it was despatched via The Great North Road to London, and possibly to Canterbury. The general poverty in the country, allied with the harsh conditions imposed by the Church, obviously caused considerable resentment among the populace in general. Robin Hood's activities in recovering some of the wealth and returning it to the local economy were naturally very popular, as were the ballads written about him.

At this time, the general belief was that all natural events, especially the Great Famine, were due to the direct actions of God, and were a divine reaction to the general sinning of mankind. This view was summed up in the following poem reckoned to date from around 1320:

> *When God saw that the world was so over proud,*
> *He sent a dearth on earth, and made it full hard.*
> *A bushel of wheat was at four shillings or more*
> *Of which men might have had a quarter before…*
> *And then they turned pale who had laughed so loud,*
> *And they became all docile who before were so proud.*
> *A man's heart may bleed for to hear the cry*
> *Of poor men who called out,*
> *'Alas! For hunger I die…!'*

Despite the desperate situation of the general population, the Church continued to demand tithes and other dues from the parishioners, and money for the purchase of indulgences. In addition, the king was claiming ever increasing amounts of tax from the land-owning barons, who of course passed the claims on to their tenants. The general failure of the prayers of the clergy and papacy to alleviate the suffering, allied to the demands from the Church for payments in one form or another, led to disillusion and resentment among the population. The population blamed the continuing hardships on corruption among the clergy and the papacy in particular. The end of the fourteenth century was a turbulent time for the Church in general. In 1384, John Wycliffe produced his English translation of the bible. This was followed shortly afterwards by the emergence of the Lollards, a religious sect regarded as heretical by the Church. The Church itself was in turmoil with the Western Schism appearing on the scene, with the papacy in the absurd position of having two popes.

There can be no doubt that before the emergence of Martin Luther, Wycliffe and the Lollards there were in existence groups of discontented people, not necessarily members of the clergy or religious activists, who were angered by the fact that during this time of unprecedented hardship the Church was further impoverishing the poorer members of the population, and sending the wealth they were collecting to the papacy in Rome. It was in this atmosphere of religious ferment that Robin Hood was active. It is little wonder that he developed an acute hatred toward the Church and its clergy and officials, clearly expressed in his directions to Little John and his companions as reported in stanza 15 of the *Gest*:

These bisshoppes and these archebishoppes
Ye shall them bete and bynde

These bishops and these archbishops
You shall beat and bind them;

Although, he is renowned as a highway robber, it is noticeable that almost, if not all, of his victims were clergy or church officials transporting their ill-gotten wealth from the North of England to London, presumably for onward transmission to Rome, the home of the papacy.

Although Jewish and Islamic communities were tolerated in parts of Europe, in general the only accepted religion in England was the Roman Catholic Church, which itself was facing turbulent times. Pope Boniface in 1302 issued a papal bull known as the Unam Sanctam, which declared that the pope had complete authority over everyone, including all rulers and kings and if they failed to carry out his wishes, they would immediately on their death descend to Hell. This was followed by an extended period of tension between the Church and the State causing a period of uncertainty in Rome. Pope Clement V who followed Boniface was French and to escape the turmoil in Rome moved to Avignon in southern France. In 1378, Pope Gregory XI returned to Rome. However, after his death, the cardinals disagreed on the appointment of his successor, with the result that two popes were elected: the Italian pope Urban VI who remained in Rome, and the French candidate Clement VII, who returned to Avignon. The two popes each excommunicated the other's followers. This situation when there were two popes lasted for around forty years and became known as the Western or Great Schism, although the term Great Schism was also applied to the earlier division between the Eastern and Western Churches in 1054.

Having established the political and religious situation which existed during Robin Hood's lifetime, it is necessary to investigate, as far as is possible, who he was. He was also known as Robin of Loxley. There was a village of Loxley which has now been absorbed into Sheffield, and local legend has it that Robin was born here and lived here, until he moved to Wakefield. In his survey of the Manor of Sheffield written in 1637, John Harrison, when describing Loxley, refers to: *Little Haggas Croft wherein is ye foundation of a house or cottage where Robin Hood was borne.*

Little Haggas Croft is described as being on the edge of Loxley Moor. As Loxley is only seventeen miles from Wakefield, but almost twice as far from Nottingham this seems possible. However, it should be noted that Harrison is only reporting on an oral legend which was three-hundred years old at the time and Robin Hood was a common name or alias.

For almost all of Robin's life, England was at war with Scotland. The war, known as the Scottish War of Independence, was in fact two separate conflicts. The first war began with an English invasion of Scotland in 1296 and lasted until 1328, and the second war began four years later and ended in 1357. During the time when Robin was active in Barnsdale there were no less than eleven separate battles, six of them taking place on Scottish soil, the remainder in the north of England. Generally, the war consisted of plundering raids on towns and villages in the north of England by the Scots, ably led by Robert the Bruce and William Wallace.

Obviously Robin, as an outlaw, was not involved in any of the battles or skirmishes but because the warfare imposed a drain on the nation's finances, the king had to impose heavy taxes on his barons which of course filtered down through every layer of society.

The final catastrophe was the outbreak of the Black Death in 1348 which together with the loss of life due to the Great Famine resulted in the deaths of about forty percent of the population of the Barnsdale region of Yorkshire, possibly including that of Robin himself.

Chapter 4
Maps and Routes

Maps provide a very reliable and easily accessed source of information, which appears to have been largely ignored by other commentators on the history of Robin Hood. In this study, the author has made full use of the ordinary Ordnance Survey maps, the Ordnance Survey map of Roman Britain, the Paris (Matthew not the town) map, the Gough Map, the Belvoir Map, various maps by John Ogilby and Jeffery's 1771 map of Yorkshire.

Reference was also made to the Geological Survey maps of the British Isles and the 1/50,000 geological map of Wakefield, which includes Wentbridge and most of Barnsdale. The book *Medieval Roads and Tracks* by Dr Paul Hindle[1] has also been extensively referred to, with particular attention to his comments on the Gough Map (map 1) and his analysis of the journeys of king Edward II.

The geological maps and the contours on the ordinary OS maps were used to confirm and consolidate local knowledge of the topography with particular reference to the discussion on the location of Barnsdale and the alleged Lancashire connection.

As mentioned above it is generally accepted that Robin Hood acted as a footpad or highway robber whose modus operandi was to waylay travellers on the main road from York to London, although his activities were generally restricted to relieving members of the clergy of money or treasure. There are conflicting claims as to whether this occurred in Sherwood Forest or in the area known as Barnsdale. It is obvious that an investigation of the roads existing in the area at the time could well give an indication of the most likely location.

The earliest map which provides any useful information is one of five produced by Matthew Paris, a monk of St Albans, about the year 1250AD. Prior to this, because there were no restrictions on where travellers could go, they only needed to know the relative positions of the various towns. The route itself was usually given as a list of place names. However, on his fifth map Matthew Paris depicted the actual route for a journey from Dover to Newcastle-on-Tyne.

The route between York and London recorded in map form by Matthew Paris lies some distance to the east of Nottingham and Sherwood Forest. The map is of a route running the full distance from Dover to Newcastle on Tyne. It does not actually pass through York, following instead the Roman road which passes ten miles west of the city through Boroughbridge and Northallerton. There are four copies of the map in existence, some showing slight variations in the neighbourhood of the Vale of Belvoir. The route north from London passes through Northampton, Stamford, crosses the River Trent at Newark and proceeds to Blyth and Doncaster before crossing the River Aire near Pontefract.

The Gough Map (map 1) is drawn on parchment made from two goat skins and is preserved in the Bodleian library in Oxford. It is not known how or when the map was made, or by whom, although an examination of the script showing place names indicates it was drawn around 1355–1366AD and has been amended on several occasions. The map is named after a previous owner rather than the map maker who is unknown. It not only shows the large and important towns, but also many, sometimes quite small settlements. Although, the medieval names of the towns are written on the map in Latin, the modern English versions of the major settlements are available on the digitised version of the map on the internet.

The map Is claimed to be the earliest map showing the roads in Britain. The routes are depicted on the map by thin red lines. Although exact road-lines are not shown, they are depicted as straight lines between the major towns on the route. It is a simple matter to determine the general route of each of the roads. The distances in miles between major towns are shown in Roman numerals alongside the roads but the miles used vary in length depending to a certain extent on the location. Thirteen main routes and nine secondary routes together with some local routes in Lincolnshire and Yorkshire are shown. The total length of roads depicted on the map is almost three thousand miles. About twelve hundred miles of the roads shown on the map are located on the line of earlier Roman roads.

A feature of both the Gough map and the Belvoir map is that east is shown at the top of the map as drawn, as that was the direction towards Jerusalem. Due to this unusual orientation of the Gough Map extracts, care should be taken when viewing them.

Although the Roman roads were constructed before the collapse of the Roman Empire, which occurred about a thousand years before the map was drawn; they were obviously still in use.

After the Roman conquest, the Romans required a road system which would enable them to speedily move large numbers of troops around the country, to deal with any uprising by rebellious Britons. The Romans were experienced road builders, and had large numbers of soldiers who were able to force the subjugated Britons to provide the necessary labour. Often their roads followed the previous track-ways or followed the same principles in keeping to the higher ground. The Roman road called Ermine Street, follows the Magnesian Limestone ridge north of Doncaster before descending to the lower ground at Barnsdale Bar. Here the Romans built an artificial embankment in Barnsdale which is still named on the Ordnance Survey maps as Roman Ridge.

After the collapse of the commercial Roman occupation of the country, the maintenance of the roads was neglected; however they had been so well constructed, and were in most cases stone paved, that they continued in use for a further thousand years and in many cases even longer.

It is interesting that, despite the obvious importance of Nottingham, the Gough Map does not show any routes passing through the town or through Sherwood Forest. Based on detailed information from another source however, it is clear that a route did exist from Nottingham through Mansfield and on to Doncaster.

There is an important item of information on the Gough Map which is not connected with roads. Towards the end of the fourteenth century, when the map was produced, there were over sixty royal forests in England, but of these the locations of only four are shown on the map. These are the New Forest, the Forest of Dean, Sherwood Forest and Inglewood Forest. The implication of this, as far as Robin Hood is concerned, is that Sherwood Forest must have been very well known, not just locally but also nationally.

The Belvoir Map, which is owned by the Duke of Rutland and held at Belvoir Castle is the oldest surviving map of Sherwood Forest, and is dated about the same time as the Gough Map. Although, the map does not show roads, it seems unlikely that such an important feature as the Great North Road would have been omitted if it did in fact run through the Forest, as claimed in some of the commercially oriented websites.

John Ogilby was born in Scotland in November 1600 and at the end of the seventeenth century he was appointed "His Majesty's Cosmographer and Geographic Printer". The following year he produced the "Britannia" atlas, a series of maps showing a number of long-distance routes through England, Wales and into Scotland. Each route was divided into sections whose lengths varied but were approximately fifty to seventy miles in length, and each section was depicted as a strip showing towns, villages and physical features at a scale of one inch to one mile. The Britannia atlas contains a series of one hundred maps printed on paper. Although published more than three hundred years after the era, we are considering they show which of the medieval roads remained in use and therefore which roads were the most important.

Reference was also made to Thomas Jeffery's Map of Yorkshire. Thomas Jeffery was geographer to King George III and produced the first accurate map of Yorkshire at a scale of one inch to one mile. Although he died in 1771, the map was not published until the following year. Despite this, the map is known as "Jeffery's 1771 Map of Yorkshire". An extract of Jeffery's Map showing the area around Barnsdale Bar is included as map 3. It should be noted that the name Barnsdale Bar does not appear on the map as the word "Bar" refers to the toll gate erected towards the beginning of the nineteenth century when the road from Barnsdale to Leeds was completed as a turnpike.

The earliest map which shows the roads in Sherwood Forest is John Chapman's map dated 1774. This map is almost 100 years later than the Ogilby Map referred to above and does not give any reliable guidance to the conditions at the time of Robin Hood.

In his book, *Medieval Roads and Tracks* Dr Paul Hindle has analysed the journeys undertaken by King Edward II. As the king would have been accompanied by a large retinue including a number of carts and wagons, Dr Hindle has assumed that he would not have followed any lesser tracks but would have confined his travels to the major routes. Rather than attempting to establish the exact lines of the various routes Dr Hindle's aim was to demonstrate the network of roads in existence in England during the medieval period. The maps he has produced consist of straight lines linking the node points of the network, which are, of course, the major towns. By comparing these maps with a straightforward geographical map, it is a relatively simple matter to deduce the major routes and the towns served and hence the approximate line of the road.

Prior to the Roman Conquest, there was a network of tracks covering most of the country. In general, these tracks followed higher ground to avoid low-lying marshy areas and areas liable to flooding. Prime examples are The Ridgeway which follows the chalk outcrop of the Berkshire Downs and Icknield Way which follows the Chiltern Hills.

These were generally routes followed by traders with their pack animals, and drovers taking animals to larger settlements, and consisted mainly of the tracks left by the travellers. No one was responsible for the maintenance and upkeep of these tracks but it was generally accepted as a pious and charitable act by local churches and congregations. Occasionally, where conditions demanded, such as in very soft and wet ground, timber wattles or even just tree branches would be placed on the ground surface to facilitate travelling. The churches and religious houses also accepted the onus of building bridges and causeways in their locality.

The only incidents of Robin Hood waylaying travellers mentioned in the *Gest,* involved members of the clergy carrying goods or money from York to London. For this reason, the roads that concern us most are those which run south from York to London. The Gough Map produced approximately one hundred years after the Paris Map shows a major route between York and London, generally in agreement with the Paris Map. The route shown on the Gough Map, apart from the section between Northampton and Stamford, coincides with the route shown on the Paris Map and is believed to be the first representation of part of what was to become known later as the Great North Road.

The River Aire forms a significant barrier to north-south travel so most routes, including any which passed through Sherwood Forest or Nottingham, either used ferries to cross the river, or more often used the Roman ford or later a bridge at Castleford. The route then passed through Pontefract and Doncaster. Later in 1198AD a timber packhorse bridge was constructed at Ferrybridge, some four miles east of the Roman ford but closer to the limestone ridge at this point. The marshy land on the north side of the river, known here as Brotherton Marsh, was also much narrower at this point than the marshes at Castleford.

Around the end of the thirteenth century the Bishop of Durham offered indulgences to anyone providing labour, materials, or other support for the construction of a causeway across Brotherton Marsh, together with a six arch stone bridge across the river which replaced the timber packhorse bridge at Ferrybridge. Although the route of the Great North Road was diverted for some distance, it was still necessary when travelling south after crossing the River Aire at Ferrybridge, to pass through Pontefract and Doncaster.

Although, neither the Paris Map nor the Gough Map show a route through Sherwood Forest, Paul Hindle on a map in his book on medieval roads shows a straight line which seems to indicate a road between Nottingham and Doncaster. However it must be born in mind that his book is about the network of roads and generally shows straight lines between the different node points on the network, rather than the actual road line.

It may be significant that neither the Paris Map nor the Gough Map show roads, main or secondary, passing through Nottingham or Sherwood Forest but both of them show the eastern route crossing the River Trent at Newark and with no connection to Nottingham. Apart from Nottingham itself there are a number of important towns and settlements located within, or close to the forest, including Newark, Southwell, Mansfield, Clipstone and Edwinstowe which must have been interconnected.

There must therefore have been a network of tracks linking them together, but obviously not main routes from York to London, although there are detailed records of a number of journeys made by the Warden and Fellows of Merton College, Oxford, to the north of England. Their route ran from Oxford to Leicester, Nottingham, Mansfield, Worksop, Blyth, Doncaster, Pontefract and York.

Clearly, there was a route through Sherwood Forest and Nottingham although this would not have been a main route, but if this route was followed from York southwards it would have necessitated travelling through Barnsdale before reaching Sherwood. Also the finishing point at Oxford lies some forty-five miles west of the more direct eastern route, thus adding considerably to the journey time. It seems the most logical connection between this route and the Great North Road would be a link between Stamford and Nottingham.

In 1306, shortly before Robin Hood is recorded as being active, William de Lamberton, Bishop of St Andrews, Robert Wishart, Bishop of Glasgow, and Henry Abbot of Scone, having been captured at the Battle of Methven in Scotland, were transported south from Newcastle to Winchester and Porchester. The route chosen passed through Pontefract, Doncaster, Tickhill, Newark and Nottingham. This route from Doncaster to Nottingham was ten miles longer than the more direct route through Mansfield and Sherwood Forest, but was taken for the greater security provided by the castles at Tickhill and Newark. It is interesting that the escort had to be increased for the part of the route through Barnsdale because of the activities of the outlaws there.

Even as late as the fourteenth century the main roads being used in Britain were the Roman Roads. The Gough Map shows the nearest Roman roads to Sherwood Forest are the road north from Derby to Chesterfield which at its nearest runs five miles west of the forest's western boundary, and the Fosse way which is about two miles from its south eastern border. This point however is far too close to Nottingham itself for outlaws to operate in safety. On the other hand, the Gough Map and others do show the former Roman Road called Ermine Street (also referred to at the time as Watling Street) running through the centre of Barnsdale.

Of the one hundred Ogilby maps only one show a route passing through Sherwood Forest and this route runs from Oakham to Nottingham then via Mansfield and Barnsley to Rotherham. It has to be remembered that this map was produced some considerable time after Robin Hood's exploits. A brief glance at the Gough Map and at Hindle's Map of the journeys by Edward II clearly shows the majority of the routes in England are located on the eastern side of the country. Hindle's Map in particular also reveals that London and York are, as would be expected, major hubs of the route network. The Gough Map also shows a route which runs north from York to Ryedale. This route is also indicated on the Hindle map which also shows it was travelled at least twice by king Edward II.

Doncaster is also sited at the crossing of two main routes between York and the southwest and between London and the northwest.

To the west of Sherwood Forest the Gough Map shows a route passing through Coventry, Coleshill, Lichfield, Derby and Chesterfield to join the eastern route at Doncaster but this, of course, entails an even longer journey.

As the axis of the country is north south and with the Peak District and the Pennines forming a barrier along the axis there is a paucity of east-west routes in the north of England. In this discussion of the accuracy of the *Gest,* we have considered the supposed Lancashire connection described in the Gest and concluded it did not exist. In his book "Robin Hood", Holt includes a map showing a route running west from Bradford across a very inhospitable section of the southern Pennines via Haworth to Colne with a link west to Skipton. On the other hand, Gough shows a direct route which follows the Aire valley from Bradford to Skipton and thence via Settle to Kirkby Lonsdale.

The Gough Map shows additional cross Pennine routes from Leeming to Kirkby Lonsdale and via Bowes and Brough to Penrith. Ogilby shows one route from Bradford to Warrington and one from Boroughbridge via Skipton and Settle to Lancaster. The Ogilby maps, of course, are dated at the end of the seventeenth century, some four hundred years later than the time we are considering but are included to show that the medieval routes were still in use and few alternative routes had been added.

Chapter 5
The Ballads

There are no reliable historical records of Robin Hood's actions. As a result we largely have to rely for information on the many poems and ballads which have been passed down to us over the last six or seven hundred years. There are a large number of these ballads and as mentioned in the prologue the fact that a document, however reliable itself, includes the name Robin Hood, or one of the several variations, is no guarantee that it refers to the individual being considered here. In view of the doubts about their veracity, it could be argued that they should be excluded from the present study as we are trying to establish the true facts about his life. However as they provide a certain amount of information, in some cases very relevant information, it would not be appropriate to ignore them completely.

In the eighteenth and nineteenth centuries, it became fashionable for writers to produce collections of ballads or even to compose new stories about Robin. As the ballads evolved and developed over the years they will be considered as a complete group with particular attention to those generally considered to be the earliest. These are included in the collections made by Thomas Percy in the late seventeenth century, Joseph Ritson in 1832 and Francis James Child in 1883. It was finally decided to look at the ballads included in the collection called *The Robin Hood Garlands and Ballads* published in 1850 by John Mathew Gutch, William Hone, Francis Douce and Edward Francis Rimbault, which is based on the Ritson collection and is complete with comments.

The book *The Robin Hood Garlands and Ballads* contains fifty-four poems or ballads, but it is not the intention to comment on all of them here. It is more appropriate for experts in medieval literature to analyse them in detail. Here we shall merely comment on their overall pattern and extract such information as considered useful in establishing the true facts. Of the fifty-four poems ten are assessed as providing no such useful information. Of the remainder, twenty-one provide accounts of Robin fighting with casual passers-by he meets during his travels, and of those fights he loses ten. It may be significant that he is not recorded as robbing a single traveller who is not a clergyman, but he robs five who are clerics of varying degrees. Not only does he steal considerable amounts of money and goods from them, but he also goes out of his way to humiliate them.

Admittedly, the poem "Little John and the Four Beggars" describes how Little John stole money from four beggars who were pretending to be disabled, and "Robin Hood and the Butcher" describes how Robin tricked the Sheriff of Nottingham out of three hundred pounds, but neither of these incidents can be regarded as robbing travellers. Neither of these incidents is described in the *Gest*.

Ten of the poems give Robin's location as being in Sherwood Forest and only eight in Barnsdale, but it should be noted that his location in Barnsdale is given in the earlier poems and references to Sherwood are only contained in the later ballads, which were possibly written some two hundred or more years after the time he is considered as being active. As described elsewhere, Sherwood Forest and Nottingham were much more widely known at the time than Barnsdale.

It is generally accepted that the earliest of the ballads is "Robin Hood and the Monk", although the most important is undoubtedly "A Lytell *Gest* of Robin Hood". There is a great deal of debate about the nature of the *Gest*; whether it is by and large a true, but somewhat enhanced record of actual events, or whether it was intended purely as entertainment to be provided as an oral presentation by a minstrel. As described below the description of the local topography is accurate, with no attempt to conceal locations by using false place names. The accuracy and detail of the descriptions make it clear that the composer of the *Gest* must have been a local resident. As such he would have been well aware of reports and stories of local events, which fact lends credibility to the accounts in the *Gest* of Robin's activities. Initially the ballads would probably have enjoyed popularity in an area restricted to Barnsdale, but as there was widespread hostility towards the Church their reputation and acceptance would have spread quite rapidly throughout the country and even into Scotland.

A considerable number of the ballads were clearly composed for purely entertainment purposes and are intended to amuse and entertain an audience or readers. Others appear to be an accurate record of places and events, changed in some respects during the passing of time, to reflect popular taste and occasionally incorporate local references. As mentioned in the prologue, this present treatise is an attempt to extract a portrait of the man on whose life and actions the ballads were based, rather than to identify a particular individual.

For reasons given above this study is mainly based, like many others, on the ballad "A *Lytell Gest of Robin Hood"*, not only because the *Gest* is one of the earliest and is also the basis of many other versions of the story, but also because the description of the topography of the Barnsdale locality is so accurate.

An example of an accurate description is the portrayal of the unnamed castle in Stanza 309. Other places such as Barnsdale, Sayles, Wentbridge, Doncaster, Blyth and St Mary's Abbey to name but a few, are clearly identified.

Stanza 21 of the *Gest* describes how Robin and his men encounter a knight on the road at Wentbridge who is later identified as Sir Richard at the Lee. When the *Gest* was composed, the word "lee" could be applied to land that had remained fallow or uncultivated but most likely referred to a glade lying within woodland.

The expression "at the lee" could therefore describe someone who dwelt on the moors

or in a woodland glade rather than in a particular village. This interpretation is confirmed in descriptions included in at least nine of the ballads analysed. For example, it is clear from the first stanza of the ballad "The Bold Pedlar and Robin Hood" that the word lee is not the name of a village or hamlet.

There chanced to be a pedlar bold,
A pedlar bold he chanced to be;
He rolled his pack all on his back,
*And he came tripping o'er the **lee.***

This interpretation is confirmed in the final stanza of the ballad,

'Robin Hood and the Bishop,

O who is yonder, quoth Little John,
*That now comes over the **lee**?*

An arrow at her I will let flie,

So like an old witch looks she.'

The glossary to volume 2 of Ritson's collection of Robin Hood ballads gives the meaning of "lee" as "plain".

In some of the ballads where the word lee is introduced it is spelled ley rather than lee. This alternative spelling is defined in the *Shorter Oxford English Dictionary* as "Land that has remained untilled for some years". It seems that Holt[1] and many others were completely mistaken in assuming that the word "lee" necessarily referred to the name of a village or hamlet. This analysis is confirmed by the format of the wording. If Lee had been the name of a village, it would be expected that the knight's name would be Sir Richard at Lee or Sir Richard of Lee, similar to Guy of Gisborne.

Some authors of books about Robin Hood even misquoted from the *Gest* to justify their own version of the story. It is also clear from the above consideration of the meaning and use of the word "lee" that it is most unlikely to be a personal or family name as assumed by many authors.

In addition to the *Gest,* the contents of other ballads, namely "Robin Hood and the Potter", "Robin Hood and the Monk" and "Robin Hood and Little John" have also been considered, as it is believed they are early examples and contain important references to location.

The Lytell Gest of Robin Hood

Stanzas 1 to 16 of the *Gest* give a general introduction to an audience, set the scene in Barnsdale, introduce Robin as a courteous yeoman and also introduce Little John, Will Scarlet and Much the Miller's son. They describe Robin's modus operandi, his religious conviction and his devotion to Mary but do not make it clear whether this refers to Mary the Virgin or Mary Magdalene.

In reply to Little John's question, Robin instructs the others not to attack husbandmen, ploughmen, good knights and squires, but only to rob bishops and archbishops, and also to beware of the Sheriff of Nottingham. This clearly sets the scene for his antagonism towards the established church and the clergy.

Robin sends Little John, Will Scarlet and Much the Miller's Son to Wentbridge and Watling Street and instructs them to look out for some traveller who they can approach and invite to meet him and perhaps join him for dinner. The *Gest* describes how they meet a knight who looks particularly depressed, travelling along a "secret track". At Wentbridge, the road descends very steeply to cross the river Went before climbing an equally steep gradient after the crossing. Because the valley sides were densely wooded and the gradients are so steep, it is likely that the road would have split into a number of multiple tracks among the trees, any one of which could be concealed from an onlooker.

The knight points out that he is on his way south, and is planning to dine at Blyth or Doncaster but nevertheless he accepts the invitation.

After they have dined and the knight prepares to go on his way, Robin asks him to pay for the meal. This appears to be the only record in the *Gest* where, despite his instructions not to steal from knights, Robin tries to extort money from a traveller who is not a member of the clergy. But the knight explains he has no money and he has had to borrow four hundred pounds to repay a debt incurred by his son. The money is owed to the rich abbot of Saint Mary's Abbey in York and has to be repaid immediately, or all his lands which have been pledged for security will be forfeit.

Because he has an intense dislike of the Church and its activities Robin agrees to lend the knight four hundred pounds on condition it is repaid within twelve months. He also gives the knight clothes, equipment, a horse and tells Little John to accompany him as his squire. The motive behind Robin's generosity was, needless to say, not purely altruistic, because the money for the loan had obviously been taken earlier as it was being transported south from the self-same abbey in York. He would have simply regarded it as another blow in his ongoing battle against the Church.

Twelve months later as the time for the knight to repay his debt to the abbot approaches, the abbot, his lawyer and his companions are celebrating because they know the knight will be unable to make the payment from his own resources. When the knight finally arrives, he claims he cannot pay and asks for more time which the abbot refuses, whereupon the knight produces the money lent to him by Robin.

Stanza 126 of the *Gest* describes how the knight, having repaid the Abbot of St Mary's in York, returns home rejoicing to Verysdale. This is the only reference to Verysdale and Sir Richard's home in the *Gest*. There is no indication in the *Gest* where Verysdale is located in England, if indeed it is within this country. However Holt has assumed for no apparent reason that Verysdale is in fact Wyresdale, a river valley on the western flank of the Forest of Bowland in the county of Lancashire.

Bellamy[12] quotes Holt and says he believes Verysdale was obviously Wyresdale, and Baldwin[11] claims that "Verysdale [is] a place usually identified with Wyresdale". Bellamy[13] enters a long discussion on various earlier versions of the explanation of the identity of Verysdale. In 1852, Ritson proposed that the name was possibly Utersdale, a suggestion followed by Hunter. It is not known where the letter "t" came from but if it is omitted Ritson's version becomes Uresdale.

It seems that Wyresdale was known as such early in the thirteenth century, so if Holt is correct in his assumption there does not appear to be a logical reason for the name Verysdale to be introduced. The possibility that it may have been due to changes in the English alphabet was examined.

The use of the letter "W" was looked into and the fact that it was quite commonly used is clearly evident from the second and fourth lines of the second stanza of the *Gest*:

> *Robyn was a prude outlaw,*
> *Whyles he walked on grounde;*
> *So curteyse an outlawe as he was one*
> *Was never non founde.*

There seems to be no simple reason therefore, why the composer of the *Gest* should include the word Verysdale instead of simply Wyresdale.

In many cases in medieval English, the letters "u" and "v" were considered interchangeable, the decision as to which letter was used seems to have been quite arbitrary. Furthermore, according to the Shorter English Dictionary, Capital V continued to be used for both "V" and "U" into the 17th cent'. Therefore when the *Gest* was being written and first printed the name "Uresdale", the valley of the River Ure, could not have been written in any form other than "Veresdale".

Until Samuel Johnson published his dictionary in 1755 there was no standardised form of spelling in the English language. Generally, words were spelled phonetically so the spelling of any given word could even have varied according to a local dialect. As a result the name of the river was recorded as either Ure or Yore. On a map of the city of Ripon, included as an inset on Jefferey's 1771 map, both names are shown alongside each other. Later, in the seventeenth century, the name Ure became accepted as the name of the river although the valley became known as Wensleydale, after the main market town in the valley, the only Yorkshire dale named after a town rather than its river.

In fact, the name "Yoredale" is preserved to the present time in the term "The Yoredale Series" used by geologists to describe the alternating beds of limestone, sandstone and marls occurring noticeably on the hills Inglebrough and Penyghent. These alternating beds of hard and softer rocks have created the waterfalls in the River Ure and its tributaries; the best known of which are Hardrow Force and the Aysgarth Falls.

Wensleydale is a long, open and broad dale, gently rising to the flat-topped hills that enclose it and give it its individual character, until the beginning of the eighteenth century the name Yoredale or Uredale after its river, the Ure, persisted alongside the name Wensleydale until the middle of the eighteenth century.

Bedale is a small but important market town often referred to as the gateway to Wensleydale. In the fourteenth century, it had a small castle or possibly just a fortified manor house, built by Sir Bryan FitzAlan between 1270 and 1305. During his lifetime Sir Bryan was installed as the Earl of Surrey. The title later passed to the 10th Earl of Arundel in 1347.

Because the knight has not yet arrived with his payment, Robin starts to get anxious and sends some men to Watling Street to see if they can spot any travellers. Little John sees a monk travelling with a number of men, presumably an escort, so he takes him to see Robin. Robin asks the monk who he is and where he is travelling from. The monk explains he is the high cellarer from St Mary's Abbey in York. Robin tells him all about the conduct of the abbot and the loan to the knight, but the monk denies all knowledge of the scam and then lies about how much money he is carrying. When the money is counted, he is found to be transporting £800 which Robin seizes.

Later, the knight arrives to repay Robin but Robin refuses the payment on the grounds that he has already just received more than twice as much from the abbey funds.

Although, the knight should be repaying his debt to Robin, the *Gest* claims that Little John, acting as the knight's squire, comes across an archery contest, joins in and wins the prize. The sheriff of Nottingham asks him his name to which he gives a false identity. The sheriff then offers to employ him and give him a home. Little John accepts but shortly afterwards he picks a fight with the sheriff's cook. After the fight, Little John persuades the cook to go with him to join Robin, but before they do so they steal some of the sheriff's silver and more than £300 in cash, which they took with them to Robin at Barnsdale.

Little John then returns to meet the sheriff and tricks him into meeting Robin. Robin forces the sheriff to spend an uncomfortable night in the forest and then to make an oath that any time he meets Robin or his men he will assist them rather than attacking them.

The *Gest* then describes how sometime later, Robin and a number of his men travelled to Nottingham and took part successfully in an archery contest. Although the account of the archery contest is possibly fictitious and copied from earlier, totally disconnected ballads, such contests were in fact very popular. Robin and his men were identified and pursued by the Sheriff of Nottingham and some armed followers. Little John was injured by an arrow in his knee, so he was assisted by Much. Every so often Little John and Much stopped and fought a rearguard action. Although it is not stated in this passage of the *Gest*, it is clear that this pursuit started in Sherwood Forest before proceeding further north through an area known as the Dukeries into South Yorkshire.

Shortly, after entering Yorkshire they came upon a castle described in stanza 309 of the *Gest* as:

Then was there a fayre castell,
A lytell within the wode;
Double-dyched it was about,
And walled, by the rode.

And there dwelled that gentyll knyght,
Syr Rychard at the Lee,
That Robyn had lent his good, goods
Under the grene wode tree.

Then was there a fair castle,
A little way into the wood,
Double-ditched around it was,
And walled, by the Rood. (cross)And there lived that noble knight
Sir Richard at the Lee,
To whom Robin had lent his
Goods under the green wood tree.

This is the first time in the *Gest* that the knight is named as Sir Richard at the Lee.

To a reader of the *Gest* with no firsthand knowledge of the area, this could be a castle straight from Fairyland or Disneyland. However anyone who knows the area well will immediately recognise that this description of the castle can only apply to Conisbrough, which is located four miles west of Doncaster and Watling Street, and fifteen miles by road south of Wentbridge. The castle keep, is almost 100ft high, circular in plan, and has six large projecting buttresses. The river Don which probably formed the southern boundary of Barnsdale, is 400 yards to the north, whilst only 260 yards west, in the grounds of St Peter's Church, is the remains of a fourth century Anglo-Saxon preaching cross (rood). It is clear from an inspection on site that there are two defensive ditches surrounding the castle. It is not necessary, however, to visit the site as the double ditches are clearly shown on the 1:25000 Ordnance Survey map Explorer sheet 279 "Doncaster" (map 9).

The site and the remains of the castle itself are currently owned by Doncaster Metropolitan Council but the castle is maintained by English Heritage. Visitors to the castle today will find that unless they are paid-up members of English Heritage, they will have to pay an entrance fee, but this contributes to providing the steps and walkways which greatly assist them in overcoming the defensive ditches.

The use of the word fair to describe a military building like a castle seems a little unusual, but at the time Conisbrough was being constructed buildings were being used to emphasise the owner's social standing. The design was very stylish at the time and the keep is circular in plan with six massive buttresses. A feature which is quite rare in British castles.

The *Gest's* description of the castle as "fair" is confirmed by Pevsner[8] who describes it as: *The position of Conisbrough Castle above the river Don, which on the N and E cuts through a narrow valley in the Magnesian limestone, is magnificent, and the keep is in the beauty of its geometrical simplicity and of its large ashlar facing unsurpassed in England.*

This aspect of the castle's description is also confirmed in an article about the castle in the *English Heritage Members' Magazine* for July 2014.

The design of the keep at Conisbrough is almost unique in Britain, but a smaller keep of similar type and date survives at Mortemer near Dieppe in northern France, a manor also associated with the Warenne family.

Stanzas 330 to 346 in the *Gest* describe how the sheriff later captures Sir Richard and takes him to Nottingham, pursued by Robin. The sheriff's original target was Robin himself but he could not locate Robin in the greenwood, so he took Sir Richard instead. Sir Richard's wife takes a horse and rides the fifteen miles from Conisbrough to Wentbridge to warn Robin and to seek his assistance. Robin calculates that in the time taken for the lady to ride the fifteen miles, the sheriff, who is accompanied by a number of well-armed men, and is therefore travelling on foot, will have travelled some three miles from Conisbrough towards Nottingham.

Allowing for normal speeds on foot and on horseback, Robin's calculations seem feasible, confirming the assumption that the *Gest* gives an accurate description. Robin, accompanied by a number of his men, set out in pursuit. It is clear from the *Gest* that Robin is also travelling on foot and is very anxious to catch the sheriff, or to reach Nottingham as quickly as possible.

'This seuen yere, by dere worthy God,
Ne yede I this fast on fote;

This seven years, dear worthy God,
I never went so fast on foot,'

Having established that the castle described in the *Gest* is in fact Conisbrough, it becomes evident that the *Gest* has become somewhat disjointed and a large portion has been omitted. Conisbrough, although an honour in its own right, was still subject to the honour of Arundel held by Edmund FitzAlan, 9th Earl of Arundel. It is likely that Sir Edmund was in residence at Arundel which explains the presence of his eldest son, Sir Richard FitzAlan, at Conisbrough.

Times were very turbulent and life was cheap so in 1326, when Sir Edmund fell out with King Edward II, the king ordered his execution and that all his property should be seized and his title forfeited. Following his execution his son, Sir Richard became heir to the title via his uncle.

. It is recorded that a number of the lords of the manor of Bedale were FitzAlan or Stapleton who were related to them by marriage. If Richard FitzAlan was resident at Bedale Castle, possibly as Lord of the Manor, he would of course have been rendered homeless when the estates were seized. The conditions of his life after being evicted are not known, but if he was forced to live in exile on the moors or within a woodland glade, he perhaps became known at that time as Richard at the Lee. Also it has to be remembered that by the time the *Gest* was written, i.e. towards the end of the fourteenth century, Richard would have succeeded to the estate and title of the Earl of Arundel. In those circumstances, the writer of the *Gest* may well have considered it was in his own interest to conceal Richard's identity.

Edward II died in 1327 and was succeeded by Edward III, who restored the Arundel titles and properties in 1330. These then passed to Richard FitzAlan when his mother died in 1347 and which he held until his death in 1376. If this analysis is accepted, it seems likely that Sir Richard at the Lee eventually succeeded to the titles of the 10th Earl of Arundel and the 8th Earl of Surrey, together with considerable wealth and property. Shortly afterwards the Earls of Arundel added the dukedom of Norfolk to their titles through the Howard and Mowbray families and so became members of the premier English peerage.

In addition, one or two approximate dates can be attached to significant events in the story. Richard could not have repaid Robin before his family's property was restored in 1331. This was only one year after he first met Robin at Wentbridge so that meeting occurred in 1330 as did his meeting with the abbot of St Mary's in York and his return to "Verysdale". It is not surprising that Sir Richard was despondent at this time as his father had just been executed, his property seized and he had probably been rendered homeless.

According to stanzas 52 and 53 of the *Gest* the knight explains that his twenty-year-old son accidentally killed a knight of Lancaster in a joust, and he had to pay compensation. Some commentators have claimed the knight came from Lancashire but it is more likely that he was a member of the retinue of the Earl of Lancaster. The claim that Sir Richard's twenty-year-old son had killed someone in a joust is highly unlikely since Sir Richard was forty years old when his son was born, so he would have been sixty before he first met Robin. It is more likely that the Lancastrian knight was killed by Sir Richard himself or the whole story was a complete fabrication by Sir Richard to explain his penurious state.

Robin's suspicions are of course aroused and he accuses the knight of being an imposter. As described in stanza 47 of the *Gest* the Sir Richard responds by stating that his ancestors have been knights for a hundred years.

It would have been unusual for anyone to have been in a position to make such a claim during this period of high infant mortality and general hardship. However according to Robin Storey it could only have been made by members of four noble families. [11] These were the earldoms of Arundel, Devon, Oxford and Warwick. The inclusion of Arundel in this group is of course very significant in the present context.

Although, the above description of events appears perfectly logical, closer examination discloses a minor discrepancy. If Sir Richard FitzAlan was born in 1307 or thereabouts, he would have only been about twenty years old when his father was executed. Clearly he could not have had a son old enough to be taking part in jousting tournaments. It seems likely therefore that his debt was not the result of his son killing an opponent in a jousting contest, but the result of some other misfortune. It seems it was more likely compensation payable to the family of an opponent killed in a tournament by Richard himself. An event possibly deliberately concealed by the author of the *Gest*.

Stanzas 355 to 358 of the *Gest* tell the extremely unlikely story of the king travelling from Nottingham to Lancashire and searching the entire county for just one outlaw and his companion. This would have been especially the case at a time when there was a great deal of turmoil in the country.

All the passe of Lancasshyre
He went both ferre and nere
Tyll he came to Plomton Parke;
He faylyd many of his dere.
There our kynge was wont to se
Herd s many one,
He coud vnneth fynde one dere,
That bare ony good horne

All the roads of Lancashire
He went, both far and near,
Until he came to Plumpton Park –
He missed many of his deer.
There our king expected to see
Many herds, not one;

He could hardly find one deer
That bore any good horns.

The word king appears sixty times in the *Gest* but in only three instances is the king's name, Edward, identified. There were three king Edwards in the fourteenth century but the *Gest* gives no indication of which one it claims travelled to Lancashire. In his book "Medieval Roads and Tracks", Paul Hindle analyses the journeys made by King Edward I and king Edward II of England in the fourteenth century. As described above the hills and rough terrain of the Pennines and the Peak District made east-west travel very difficult in the north of England. As a result visits to Lancashire by a ruling monarch were a rare occurrence. It is clear from Hindle's maps and particularly maps 10, 11 and 12[9] that apart from Edward I's visits to Wales very few journeys were made west of the Peak District and the Pennines. Edward I passed through part of Lancashire for a very short distance near Kirkby Lonsdale and Edward II made only one visit to Lancashire when he journeyed to Liverpool in October 1323, and in his book *Edward III*, W Mark Ormrod [10] claims of Edward III:

Some parts of the kingdom and dominions remained neglected: Edward was never to set foot in Devon and Cornwall, in Cheshire and Lancashire, or in Wales, Ireland and Aquitaine.

It is clear therefore that the only royal visit to Lancashire at that time was the one made by Edward II in 1323 when he travelled from York to Liverpool by way of Ripon, Skipton, Burnley, Blackburn and Ormskirk. The composer of the *Gest* was obviously aware of this fact when incorporating the king's journey into the ballad. The king remained at Liverpool and stayed at the castle there from 24 October to 30 October. Edward II's journey through Lancashire is illustrated in map 8.

For some reason, Holt[4] claims that the obvious rendering of the name "Verysdale" is Wyresdale in Lancashire although there is no evidence in the *Gest* to support this claim. He then assumes that Sir Richard at the Lee is so named because his home is at the hamlet of Lee[3] situated in Wyresdale although it is shown above that Lee in Sir Richard's name is almost certainly not a place name.

The king's journey to Lancashire was probably necessary to deal with the rebellious barons and at the same time the Scots in the Wars of Independence, under Robert the Bruce, were making regular forays across the border.

Although not stated explicitly in the *Gest,* the impression gained when reading the section on the activities in Lancashire, is that the entire episode has been deliberately distorted to conceal the truth. This was probably done when the *Gest* was first composed, but may have happened at any time in the hundred or so years between the occurrence of the events and the printing of the *Gest.*

Holt[5] when referring to Lancashire claims that *It is the presence of the place names and the story of the king's journey together which make a common origin in Lancashire seem probable.* It has been shown above that Lee is not a place name at all, the name Wyresdale is the result of a wild guess and Plumpton Park is well known and is two and a half miles south of Knaresborough in North Yorkshire. It may also be significant that after repaying his debts at York Sir Richard returned home. If home was situated in Wensleydale, this would have involved a journey of 38 miles whereas a journey to Wyresdale would have been nearly eighty miles.

Fountains Abbey, near Ripon is only fifteen miles from Sir Richards's home at Bedale. In the Abbey, archives are records of the following payments to entertainers in the late fifteenth century.[6]

...to a blind minstrel, 6d; to the players of Topcliffe, 4d; to the Minstrel of William de Plumpton, 8d; to the boy bishop of Ripon, 3s: to a fool from Byland, 4d; to players from Thirsk, 4d; to the minstrel of the Earl of Northumberland, 8d; to a story-teller whose name was unknown, 6d; to the minstrels of Beverley, 16d; to the minstrels of Lord Arundel, 16d; ...to the boy bishop of York, 6s 8d; to the players of Ripon, 2d.

It becomes clear on following the above reference to William de Plumpton that he was a member of the Plumpton Family who held Plumpton Hall in the parish of Spofforth in North Yorkshire some three miles south east of Harrogate. Plumpton Park is clearly shown on the 1/25,000 Ordnance Survey map of Leeds – Landranger sheet 104. His death which was recorded in 1362 obviously links with the period being considered here. This is clearly the Plumpton Park referred to in stanza 357 of the *Gest* and located in Yorkshire and not in Lancashire.

After Robin and his men had been to Nottingham to rescue Richard and kill the sheriff, the king travelled to Nottingham where he was apprised of what had happened, so he immediately decided to take some of his men and try to capture Robin and Richard. Robin and Richard now realise they are wanted men so Robin persuades Richard to join him in the greenwood and live as an outlaw until such time as they can persuade the king to grant them a pardon. An interesting point arises here as Robin advises Richard to abandon his horse: clearly the outlaws normally travelled on foot.

In Stanzas 354 to 360, the *Gest* describes how the king travelled to Nottingham accompanied by several Knights and presumably with others, with the intention of capturing Robin and Sir Richard. He was unable to find them in Nottingham so he took possession of all of the knight's property. This statement in the *Gest* is probably a reference to the execution of Richards's father and the seizure of his property in 1326 as described above.

It appears he had been misled, possibly deliberately, about the whereabouts of the two he was seeking. It is claimed in the *Gest* that he had travelled to Lancashire in pursuit of Robin and the knight; however it is shown above that this is unlikely. He may have been told that the knight had property at Plumpton, a hamlet in Lancashire so he went there and according to the *Gest*, found a Plumpton Park and realised that a large number of deer had been taken. It is obvious that there is a great deal of misinformation here as there is no evidence that the king in fact visited this part of Lancashire, and there is no evidence of a Plumpton Park in Lancashire, although there is one, included in the Honour of Arundel in Sussex.

The king then tells his knights that he will give Sir Richard's property to any of them who is able to kill Sir Richard, but a wise old knight says that whilst Robin is still alive and armed, that would be as good as a death warrant. Then a forester tells the king that if he disguises himself as an abbot, and takes five of his knights disguised as monks he will take him to meet Robin. The king takes the forester's advice and disguised as an abbot goes into the greenwood with his five knights, pack horses and baggage train. Clearly, a tempting target for Robin Hood. Curiously, this appears to be the only indication in the *Gest* that Robin may have been in Sherwood Forest, as this incident is described as taking place fairly close to Nottingham. As usual Robin suggests that his guest stays awhile and points out that they only have the "king's deer" to live on. Perhaps this is a reference to the effects of the Great Famine. He then points out that the clergy have churches, rents and other income "and gold in great plenty". An indication of a feeling of resentment against the Church despite his obvious reverence for God and St Mary. Robin suggests the abbot should hand over some of the money he has with him.

The king (alias the abbot) replies by saying he has just spent two weeks in Nottingham with the king and has had to spend a lot of money. As a result he only has forty pounds with him. Robin took the forty pounds, gave half to his men and gave the rest back to the "abbot". The "abbot" then admits he has come from the king, shows Robin the royal seal, and invites Robin back to Nottingham to a feast. Robin says that in view of the invitation the abbot has just given him, the abbot should stay and dine in the greenwood. Robin's invitation is accepted. The feast is prepared and Robin summoned his men. The "abbot" is amazed as 140 of Robin's men appear all dressed in Lincoln Green and at the control Robin clearly has over them. After the meal, Robin tells the "abbot" that he will show him how they live and suggests that the next time he sees the king he should tell him, and because of his rank he should obtain instructions from him on how he should proceed. All Robin's men get up and string their bows which causes alarm among the guests.

There follows an account of an archery contest in which the price of losing is a blow on the head from the victorious opponent. Although archery contests were very popular at this time, it is likely that this report is somewhat fictitious. Finally, Robin and Sir Richard look the king intently in the face and recognise him. Robin asks for pardon both for himself and his men which the king grants and says Robin and his men should go with him to his court as servants. Robin agrees but says if he does not like the life at the king's court he will quickly return to his old way of life in the greenwood. The king and his men then dress in Lincoln green like the outlaws and return to Nottingham with them.

The king and Robin rode together towards Nottingham continuing their archery contest as they did so. It is unusual for Robin to ride as he usually travels on foot. The people of Nottingham panicked when they saw the outlaws riding into the town but their minds were put at rest when they saw the king. The description of the archery contest as they ride towards Nottingham seems to be somewhat theatrical and contrived for the benefit of the listening audience.

The king returned Sir Richard's lands and Robin thanked him for his pardon and agreed to stay at the court as the king had suggested. The whole of the preceding account of the king seizing and then returning Sir Richard's property probably relates to the known facts of the execution of the 9th Earl of Arundel and subsequent seizure and restoration of the title and property to his family.

Robin stayed at the royal court for fifteen months but was beginning to feel his age, felt trapped and was feeling depressed. All these effects were no doubt exacerbated by the lasting effects of the famine. He saw the king and said that he had made a chapel dedicated to Mary Magdalene in Barnsdale which he would like to visit. It is unlikely that he would have actually built such a chapel from scratch but there is a Norman church dedicated to Mary Magdalene at Campsall in Barnsdale, only three miles from Wentdale.

Having been involved in the construction of Askern Swimming Baths less than half a mile from Campsall church I am reasonably well acquainted with the village and the nearby "Old Bells" public house. Following Robin's claim reported in the *Gest* and Pevsner's description of the works carried out during the thirteenth and fourteenth centuries, it was obvious that I needed photographs of the church. Unfortunately on my first visit I discovered that the church only opened for Sunday services so my photography was limited to external views. However I learned that the church wardens, Mr and Mrs Jordan would be present a few days later so I returned and met them then. On my arrival, they immediately telephoned the priest in charge, Dr Richard Walton, who joined us for a very interesting and helpful chat about the church's history and local legends about Robin.

It is believed that the first church on the site at Campsall was Anglo-Saxon, of timber construction, but this was replaced shortly after the Norman Conquest by an early Norman masonry church, cruciform in layout.

Sir Nikolaus Pevsner, the eminent art and architecture historian recorded a very detailed description of the extensive repairs, alterations and extensions carried out to Campsall Church during the thirteenth and fourteenth centuries:[7]

More work was done c. 1300 or a little earlier. The most interesting piece is the W bay of the S aisle, which was given a domical rib-vault (single-chamfered ribs). There is a chamber above this vault. On the N side, the corresponding bay has a W window with a shouldered lintel and a small cusped lancet above this. In the N aisle, N wall a recess with quadrant moulding, also typical of c. 1300…It is possible that this group of events actually belongs to two phases, one about the middle, the other at the end of the century. Right in the C14, and typical of the Dec style, is the delightful S doorway with a shouldered lintel under a depressed two – centred arch…

I was particularly interested in the vaulted ceiling described by Pevsner which although very basic is unusual in a village church. My overall impression though was that what I was looking at had no doubt been observed some seven hundred years earlier by Robin Hood himself. Maybe the stones I was touching could well have been touched by him. Soon after the church was built the transepts were removed, the church itself was considerably enlarged and the rather elegant west tower constructed. Photograph 29 shows some of the extensive work carried out at this time. The entire chancel to the right of the red bins shown in the photograph was built then and it does not require an architect's eye to see the different styles on either side. The deterioration of the standard of design and workmanship between the earlier and later building work is also noticeable. Perhaps this is the result of the effects of the famine on both the physical well-being of individuals and the overall reduction of the available work force.

It is clear from the description of the work done that it amounted to virtually rebuilding a large part of the church which would have taken several years to complete. It is quite possible therefore that Robin was personally involved in the rebuilding work and his claim to have made the church might just have been an accidental or possibly even deliberate exaggeration of the facts. It is also of course possible that the word was used to suit the metre of the verse.

Some of the other ballads include claims that Robin's band included up to 300 men so it would be reasonable to assume that this would include a number of artisans such as builders and masons who could have provided the necessary skills and labour for the work.

Also it has to be remembered that the Great Famine commenced at this time and this not only resulted in a shortage of food, but also a dramatic increase in the cost of living and severe financial problems. Robin's contribution may well have been financial rather than physical. Perhaps he considered that he was justified in "releasing" some English church money as it was being transported to Rome and donating it to the building of an English church.

It cannot be coincidence that the fourteenth century claim in the *Gest* of building work at the church is supported by a description of the work made by a renowned professor of Fine Art and Architecture in the twentieth century.

It seems that this part of the *Gest* together with Pevsner's independent description of the building work at the church, and the earlier claims in the *Gest* that Robin was located in Barnsdale alongside the Great North Road, together with the onset of the Great Famine and the outbreak of the Black Death present a coherent and tenable story.

Robin tells the king he is homesick for Barnsdale. The king agrees that if that is the case, he should return but only for seven nights. However when Robin gets to Barnsdale he decides he will not return to the king's court.

The *Gest* is not a historical document but it does, however, give clues as to the passage of time so any calculation of times and dates based on the *Gest* can only be considered as an approximation. As described above it is assumed that Robin was possibly outlawed for supporting the Earl of Lancaster in his rebellion against King Edward II in 1322 and that he was outlawed along with other contrariants in 1322–23. It is of course possible that, in order to escape the consequences of his disloyalty he voluntarily adopted the status of outlawry to avoid capture or to follow his religious convictions. The first part of the *Gest* describes how Robin, now an outlaw, met Little John, Much the Miller's Son and Will Scarlet. Robin then sends them to look out for travellers on Watling Street. They meet the unidentified knight and return with him to Robin. After Robin lends the knight four hundred pounds, the knight goes to York to repay the debt he owes to the abbot of St Mary's Abbey. This action could have occupied a year.

The knight is due to repay the four-hundred-pound loan to Robin after twelve months and the *Gest* explains that Robin is becoming agitated because the repayment is delayed until the last day, which accounts for another year.

Historical records show that the king visited Nottingham in 1324 on his return from Lancashire and it is probable that, if it happened at all, the meeting between him and Robin took place at that time. During the meeting the king, disguised as an abbot, pardoned Robin and persuaded him to join the royal household. This event may be completely fictional but the description in the *Gest* gives an indication of the time scale involved.

It is reasonable to suppose that meeting Robin would not have been high on the king's list of priorities, so the meeting would probably have taken place late in 1324. If Robin did in fact fight at the battle of Boroughbridge, as others have suggested, he would have been in his early to mid-twenties when he met the king. According to the *Gest* (stanza 433) he spent fifteen months working as a member of the royal establishment and he then returned to the greenwood for twenty-two and a half years. When he left the greenwood, he would have been in his late forties and already having to take things easy, as described in Stanza 434 of the *Gest*. He would also have been feeling the effects of the ravages of the Great Famine which had reduced the population of England by ten to fifteen percent and life expectancy in England to 36 years.

By this time, the year would have been 1348, and it was in 1348 that the plague, the Black Death, struck in Yorkshire and which by 1349 had resulted in the deaths of more than a third of the remaining population. The population of Yorkshire had been almost halved in the 34 years between the onset of the Great Famine and the end of the Black Death. Clearly Robin Hood could have been one of the many victims. The plague occurred in two forms, Bubonic plague, which usually caused the death of an infected person within three to four days and the more virulent form, Pneumonic Plague, which invariably caused death within two days.

It is often claimed that the *Gest* describes how Robin travelled to Kirklees priory to be bled by the prioress and in the process she treacherously allowed him to bleed to death. The legend claims that as Robin lay on his death bed in the priory gatehouse, he called for his bow and an arrow. After shooting the arrow he asked that his body should be buried where the arrow had landed. There is a monument within the grounds of Kirklees Hall which it has been claimed marks the position of his grave. However, a survey of the area lying within a bowshot of the site of the former gatehouse was carried out. The survey, using ground penetrating radar showed no evidence of disturbed ground which would have been present if there had been a grave, however old, in the area.

At the present time, Kirklees is a metropolitan borough encompassing a large area of West Yorkshire, including Huddersfield, but there does not appear to be any indication in the *Gest* or elsewhere that this is the area referred to. The place-name used in the earlier versions of the *Gest* is Kyrkely which is probably formed from the two words kirk and lee and to have referred to uncultivated land adjacent to a church. Kirklees is located some 30 miles west of Wentbridge which would have been a considerable distance for a person in such a poor state of health to travel. It is more likely that he would have sought help from much closer to home. Pontefract was the closest sizeable town to Wentbridge and was the location of a priory and a hospital, and would have been a much more logical destination.

Originally, the modern town of Pontefract was formed from two Anglo-Scandinavian settlements located about one mile apart and known individually as Kirkby and Tanshelf. The name Tanshelf is preserved as the name of a local area of Pontefract and the town's second railway station. As described elsewhere the word lee can be applied to land which had been left fallow or uncultivated, so the name Kirklees could have been formed from the name Kirkby and the word lee denoting uncultivated or fallow land, at or near Kirkby, or land adjacent to a church as described above. The priory and hospital were both in existence before Kirkby and Tanshelf merged to become Pontefract.

Immediately, adjacent to the castle in the Kirkby area of Pontefract is All Saints Church which was part of a group of related buildings including a Cluniac priory dedicated to St John the Evangelist, and St Nicholas' Hospital. It is not clear whether the hospital pre-dated the priory but it is clear that it was well-established by the early fourteenth century. Unfortunately, neither the priory nor the hospital have survived until the present time. It is thirty miles or one days travelling from Wentbridge to the Kirklees Priory near Huddersfield which is often, probably incorrectly, regarded as the site of Robin's death, but it is less than four miles to the former St Nicholas Hospital.

Although blood-letting was one of the methods used for dealing with any disease, it is unlikely that, once the infection had struck, there would have been time for Robin to travel to Kirklees near Huddersfield and for his cousin, the prioress, and her lover Roger of Doncaster, to have laid their plans to murder him and to have made any arrangements. In any case, why bother to kill anyone when the chances of them dying from natural causes were so high.

Recently archaeologists discovered ancient graves adjacent to the site of the priory one of which may have been that of Robin, although in 1569 the historian Richard Grafton referring to Robin Hood, recorded in his *Chronicle at Large* that:

After whose death the Prioresse of the same place caused him to be buried by the high way side, where he had used to rob and spoyle those that passed that way.

This can only refer to the Great North Road at or close to Wentbridge. Later in 1622 Michael Drayton in his Poly-Olbion song 28 claims that Robin died at Kirkby.

The location of the priory as recorded in the Gest is Kyrklely which is a name likely to have been formed from a combination of kirk and lee or church and lee. That is the church and an area of uncultivated land close to a church; possibly the graveyard. Pontefract's St Nicholas' church is adjacent to a priory Kirkby and close to the Great North Road.

In the first few years of the fourteenth century, there were rumours that some of the nuns from the Kirklees Priory near Huddersfield were entertaining men, religious and otherwise, in the nunnery. As a result the Archbishop of York, William Greenfield declared the nunnery a house of disrepute. It is probable that the authors, or possibly later editors, of the *Gest* considered that Robin's death from the plague was so common-place that they combined the account of his death with the story of the nuns to embroider it with the titillating story of the fornicating prioress.

As a victim of the plague it is possible that Robin would have been buried, like so many others, in an unmarked communal grave, although it is also quite possible, in view of his often stated love of the Greenwood, that his friends buried him in the peaceful and tranquil setting of Wentdale or possibly in the hallowed ground of the graveyard at St Mary Magdalene's church at Campsall. All of these sites could be considered as being near to Sayles and the Great North Road.

The detailed record of the passage of time given in the *Gest* gives a clear indication that this part of the *Gest*, with the exception of the description of his death and burial, is a true record of events and is not fictional.

Robin Hood and the Monk

Despite the fact that Robin Hood and the Monk is believed to be one of the earliest surviving written ballads, it was not printed until about 1450 or a hundred years after Robin's death. It relates a story about Robin being recognised in Nottingham by a monk who informs the sheriff. Robin is captured by the sheriff but is later freed by Little John and Much the Miller's son. Although, one of the earliest ballads, it is considered that this story is probably fictional and has no historical importance. Whether the action as it is described is fictional or factual the ballad gives an indication of Robin's devotion to St Mary, although it is not clear if his allegiance is to Mary the Virgin or Mary Magdalene. Although, he is advised by Little John and Much the Miller's Son not to travel unescorted to Nottingham, he is determined to go to St Mary's Church to celebrate matins or mass. He ignores their advice and is captured by the sheriff but is later rescued.

It is not clear why Robin felt it was necessary to travel to Nottingham as there is a church dedicated to St Mary the Virgin at Badsworth only two miles from Wentbridge and another dedicated to St Mary Magdalene at Campsall only three miles away.

Robin Hood and the Potter

This early ballad which was written or printed about 1503, some 150 years after Robin's death, is a tale about a potter taking a cart load of pots to Nottingham to sell, when he is stopped by Robin Hood who demands payment for safe passage through the greenwood. The potter refuses and gets a quarter staff from his cart, upon which Robin draws his sword but the potter knocks it out of his hand and knocks Robin to the ground. Robin then persuades the potter to change clothes and let him take the cart and its contents on to Nottingham. At Nottingham, Robin sells most of the pots but when he has only five left, he gives them to the sheriff's wife who was so grateful she invited him to dine with the sheriff and herself. By coincidence, there is an archery contest which Robin won. The sheriff asked Robin if he had ever met Robin Hood. This ballad is of course unlikely to be a record of a factual event and was probably composed for purely entertainment reasons. It does, however, contain in the sixth stanza the line:

Y met hem bot at Wentbreg,'seyde Lytell John,

I met them both at Wentbridge said Little John.
The significance of this line is that it appears to be the only reference in the early ballads to Robin's precise location.

Robin Hood and Little John

This Ballad relates how Robin met Little John on a narrow bridge over a river. As usual neither would give way so they ended fighting each other with staves and as usual the fight ended with Robin being the loser and being dumped in the river. On emerging, he uses his horn to summon his men to come to his aid.

The narrow bridge on which Robin and Little John engaged in their quarterstaff fight would have been similar to the existing Hunters' Bridge in Brockadale and shown in Photograph number 8. It is not suggested that the present "Hunter's Bridge" is an actual replacement for the original bridge on which Robin and Little John fought, or that the location provides evidence to support the veracity of the ballad: it may of course just be a coincidence.

Only a few hundred yards from the bridge is "long Crag" which is a nearly vertical exposed rock surface forming part of Brockadale's northern valley wall.

They happen'd to meet on a long narrow bridge,
And neither of them wou'd give way;
Quoth Bold Robin Hood, and sturdily Stood,
'I'll shew you right Nottingham play.'

Then unto the bank he did presently wade,
And pull'd himself out by a thorn;
Which done, at the last, he blow'd a loud blast,
Straitways on his fine bugle-horn:
The echo of which through the vallies did flie,
At which his stout bowmen appear'd.
All cloathed in green, most gay, to be seen:
So up to their master they steer'd.

The word echo can refer to a sound reflected from a hard surface or to an identical sound repeated by a different source. If a number of Robin's supporters repeated his signal at various distances, it is quite possible that it could be heard as far away from Brockadale as five miles. In this case, the message would have reached all of his followers within an area covering eighty square miles. If they were travelling by horse, they could all have reached a meeting in Brockadale in 10 minutes or within an hour if travelling on foot.

1. C J Holt, *Robin Hood* Thames and Hudson (2011) p 95
2. Ibid. p 95
3. Ibid. p 95
4. Ibid. p 95
5. Ibid. p 98
6. Ibid. p 128
7. N Pevsner, *The Buildings of England – Yorkshire The West Riding* Yale University Press (1967) p 155
8. Ibid. p 167

9. P Hindle, *Medieval Roads and Tracks* Shire Publications Ltd. (2013) p26, 27
10. W Mark Ormrod, *Edward III* Yale University Press (2012) p 63
11. D Baldwin, *Robin Hood,* Amberley Publishing Plc., (2011) p 67
12. J G Bellamy, *Robin Hood an historical enquiry* Indiana University Press (1985) p 33
13. Ibid. p75–80

Chapter 6
Location

The earlier ballads describe Robin's location as Barnsdale; whereas later versions claim he dwelt in Sherwood Forest. To determine where he actually spent the time he was living as an outlaw, it is necessary to consider the relative merits of both Barnsdale and Sherwood Forest as considered from his point of view. Sherwood Forest was a Royal Forest lying to the north of Nottingham, with clearly defined boundaries and subject to forest laws, whereas Barnsdale or possibly Barnsdale Forest was an undefined area, generally accepted as being situated between Doncaster and Pontefract, but which may have extended over a much larger area.

As mentioned above the geology of an area has far reaching effects. These extend not only to the obvious features such as hills and valleys but also to water supply, soil types, flora and fauna and therefore to crops and agricultural productivity and hence to population density. In his book *Britain's Structure and Scenery* Stamp, [1] when referring to the Keuper and Bunter Sands and Pebble Beds, describes the soils they produce as: …so coarse and light as to be agriculturally hungry and so [are] occupied by heathland. Good examples of the latter are Sherwood Forest or the Dukeries and Cannock Chase.

On their website, the Nottinghamshire Wildlife Trust describes Sherwood Forest during the Robin Hood era as:

Centuries ago, the majority of Sherwood Forest was heathland, rather than dense oak woodland as many people believe. The heathland would have been used for grazing and burnt to help the heather plants to regenerate. This traditional management was crucial to the survival of heathland habitats, preventing them from being overgrown with trees and grasses.

Today, traditional management has ceased and since 1800, due to a combination of intensive agriculture, plantation forestry and urban development, Nottinghamshire has lost 90% of the original heathland that once covered a vast area.

The vegetation in medieval Sherwood Forest would have mainly been comprised of heather and gorse with a scattering of silver birch trees and the occasional oak tree. The phrase "under the greenwood" occurs regularly in the *Gest* but this appears to be somewhat inappropriate considering the sparse canopy which would have been provided by the flora described above. It would be difficult to take cover under a bunch of heather or a gorse bush.

The poor quality of the soils contributed to limited agricultural production so any human habitation tended to be limited, and villages and other settlements were generally small and fairly well scattered. This restriction on the size of settlements was of course emphasised after 1315 by the effects of the Great Famine. The rather sparse population and the heathland vegetation combined to provide an ideal landscape for hunting, which possibly explains the reason for the existence of the royal forest.

The soils in Barnsdale on the other hand, due to their origin from the underlying mixture of coal measure clays and sandstones, and the limestones from the Went Hills, were much more productive. The steep slopes of the limestone escarpment and the valley sides limited the areas which could be cultivated, and even made the felling of timber very difficult, resulting in the original "wildwood" remaining undisturbed as densely packed, in places almost impenetrable woodland.

The fact that Sherwood is not mentioned in the earlier ballads, and particularly in the *Gest*, has been referred to above but an incident is described in stanzas 281 to 310 in the *Gest* which could not have occurred anywhere else.

Although this incident is described above as possibly fictitious, it does form part of a coherent story and should therefore be described in some detail. As briefly described in chapter 5 above, Robin and up to seventy of his men, relying on an assurance from the sheriff that they would not be molested and no doubt dressed in their Lincoln Green uniforms, attended an archery contest in Nottingham. The sheriff reneged on his promise and Robin and his men were attacked by the sheriff and his supporters.

On being attacked, Robin and his men decided to return to the greenwood, which in this case obviously referred to Barnsdale and Wentbridge, a distance of approximately fifty miles on foot. During this journey they would of course be pursued by the sheriff and his men. There is no indication in the *Gest* or elsewhere of the delay in the sheriff departing, or the lead Robin and his men enjoyed.

Unfortunately, at some stage in the melee or during the subsequent pursuit, Little John was wounded by an arrow and so their progress was impeded, and this would have forced them to take the shortest and most direct route. As far as possible this would have been a straight line between Nottingham and Wentbridge, although it would have been necessary to make a few diversions to avoid the obvious danger areas. By this time, Robin's antagonism towards the established church would have been well known, so the danger areas would have included monasteries as well as locations where some of the sheriff's men may have been gathered.

Stanza 289 of the *Gest* sets the scene for the archery contest and the starting point for the subsequent pursuit:

Whan they cam to Notyngham,
The buttes were fayre and longe
Many was the bolde archere
That shoted with bow s stronge

When they came to Nottingham,
The butts were fair and long,
Many was the bold archer
That shot with bow so strong.

This description makes it clear that the contest was held on the Nottingham City butts which were located just outside the city walls, near the north west gate known at the time as the Bar Gate, but later renamed Chapel Bar.

As the route they were following headed almost due north they would probably have travelled via Hucknall and across the River Leen to Papplewick, known at the time as the "Gateway to Sherwood Forest". Papplewick was a very small village and it is not clear if it even had a church at that time, although a local legend claims Alan-a-Dale, one of Robin's men, is in fact buried there. The first ten miles or so of their journey would have been a steady but very gentle climb as they were making their way out of the wide valley of the River Trent. The heathland vegetation would not have significantly impeded their travel, but on the other hand would not have provided much, if any, cover from their pursuers.

Their route took them past several villages so there would have been areas where the heathland vegetation gave way to cultivated land and where villagers were probably working. In the uncultivated areas, the villagers might also have been engaged in charcoal burning, tending and burning the heather and even, just two or three miles west of the direct track, mining shallow coal seams.

Twelve miles north of Nottingham the fugitives, if they had been following their straight-line route, would have passed Newstead Priory three quarters of a mile away to the west. At the time, extensive building work was being carried out as some parts of the priory were being rebuilt and others extended. Two miles further and they would have crossed Rainworth Water and what is now a long-distance footpath known as "Robin Hood Way". There does not appear to be any connection with the outlaw but it seems there are people determined to add Robin's name to any feature in the area which does not actually move.

Their path now passes close to Mansfield and Mansfield Woodhouse. Mansfield would have been the largest town on their route so they would have avoided it. Such a diversion would probably have been unnecessary in the case of Mansfield Woodhouse since it is likely that it had not been completely rebuilt following the disastrous fire in 1304. Whether or not they passed through Mansfield itself they would have crossed the River Maun. Almost four miles east on the banks of the river was the building known as King John's Palace, which was a royal residence visited by king Edward II in 1315. Clearly, a place to be avoided. Two miles further east was Rufford Abbey which in view of Robin's reputation as an antagonist of the established church was also a place to avoid. Robin would no doubt have in mind the fact that in 1271 Roger Godberd, who is described in chapter 1, was captured by the sheriff in the grounds of the Abbey.

It is obvious that Robin and his men would have had to choose their route carefully at this point in their journey. About two miles further on they would have crossed the River Meden, which was not only the northern boundary of the Forest but also the boundary between Nottinghamshire and Derbyshire.

From here, the travellers continue northward into the area known as the Dukeries, so called because there are five ducal estates within a fairly limited area, but none of them are close enough to Robin's proposed route to have had any effect on his planning. From here on, the ground becomes slightly more hilly and less populated despite the presence of the large ducal estates.

The next eight and a half miles of their trek lay through part of Derbyshire, passing close to the village of Shirebrook and crossing the River Poulter at Langwith. The last village on their route before passing into the West Riding of Yorkshire at Bondhay Dyke would have been Whitwell.

The first village they would have arrived at in Yorkshire is South Anston. Unusually the church here had no tower or spire. Two- and three-quarter miles further north the church at Laughton-en-le-Morthen was also constructed without a tower or spire but both tower and spire were added in 1377. A short distance north-east of Laughton lay the Cistercian Roche Abbey, a place Robin probably considered it would be advisable to avoid.

Although, the ground level did not exceed 500 feet above sea level, the terrain had become decidedly more hilly and walking more difficult as Robin approached Maltby.

As they approached the high ground close to Braithwell or the site of the modern hamlet of Micklebring situated on a bluff overlooking Conisbrough Parks, they may have been able to see for the first time since leaving Nottingham, the top of the keep of Conisbrough Castle. From this point, the castle is only three miles distant and almost due north. The castle is described in detail above, in chapter 5 "The Ballads".

As mentioned above many people believe that Sherwood Forest was dense woodland and that Robin would have been travelling through this kind of countryside. In fact for the first part of his journey from Nottingham, as far as Mansfield the vegetation would have been mainly heathland. From Mansfield to near Braithwell, the underlying rocks are limestone and the vegetation would change from heathland to mainly open grassland. The *Gest* gives no clues as to the time of year when this incident occurred, but in summer the grass would no doubt have included a fairly dense carpeting of wild flowers and supported a number of grazing domestic animals.

Finally as he passed Braithwell and descended the scarp slope only two or three miles from Conisbrough, Robin would have passed onto the coal measures, the soils derived from which, easily support trees and dense woodland. It is here that Robin would have entered the natural woodland (A lytell within the wode) although it is quite possible that Robin's view of the castle was obstructed by the trees even though it was only two and a half miles away.

Several commentators, including J C Holt[2] and D Baldwin[3], when trying to identify the mysterious, fair castle seem to have forgotten, or have ignored the fact that the word "forest" in Old English referred to an area subject to forest laws and was in no way related to the vegetation. The word "wood" or "greenwood" referred to land supporting the growth of trees. The line within the *Gest* describing the castle as being "A lytell within the wode" has generally been assumed to mean a short distance within Sherwood Forest, whereas it is actually referring to a location within the woodland just south of Conisbrough Castle. It is obvious that Conisbrough is the castle described in the *Gest* as it fits the description exactly and is absolutely unique in the country.

The *Gest* gives the impression that Robin and his men were surprised to arrive at the castle, although they must have been very well aware of its existence lying as it does, only fourteen miles from Wentbridge. Even so its appearance would have been, and still is, awe inspiring. The effect on the sheriff's men would have been even more overwhelming. They must have realised immediately the impossibility of besieging the castle. They had travelled on foot a distance exceeding forty miles. It would have been impossible for them to have transported siege engines, and cannons were only just making an appearance and in any case would have been no more effective against the fifteen feet thick castle walls than their bows and arrows. It is not surprising they withdrew after forty days.

In their attempts to justify their suggestions that the Robin Hood legend is based on the earlier exploits of Roger Godberd, both Holt and Baldwin have written at some length about Fenwick Castle. Fenwick was in fact a moated and crenelated manor house and is only described as a castle in one document. Baldwin attempts to link Fenwick with the castle described in stanza 309 of the *Gest* but is unable to do so. He then describes at length why he considers Wellow (later known as Jordan) is the castle described in the *Gest*. In the *Gest,* the castle is described as:

Then was there a fayre castell,
A lytell within the wode;
Double-dyched it was about,
And walled, by the rode.

Baldwin assumes the wood referred to is Sherwood Forest, ignoring the difference between a wood and a forest, and he then points out that in fact Wellow is close to, but is not in fact within the forest. Furthermore, "Rode" was the early spelling of "rood", the name used for the cross on which Christ was crucified, but Baldwin translates it as "road". "Road" did not gain its present meaning of thoroughfare until the late sixteenth century.

Bellamy[4] suggests that the castle could be Annesley castle located within Sherwood Forest and about eight miles from Nottingham. Like Holt and Baldwin, Bellamy has assumed that the word "wode" refers to the forest rather than a wood.

The official status and extent of Barnsdale are not clear, although it is believed that it was occasionally used by the king or selected nobles for hunting. It is interesting to compare how Barnsdale and Sherwood Forest are treated in the ballads. As far as Barnsdale is concerned the ballads, and the Gest in particular are very precise. Reference is made to the village of Wentbridge, the Sayles and Watling Street. There is an obvious link to Conisbrough and through the various maps to the Great North Road.

Barnsdale is a few miles further from Nottingham, the Sheriff of Nottingham's base than Sherwood Forest, and as Robin and his men were relying on relieving certain travellers of their wealth, it would also have been necessary to find a location relatively close to one or more major roads. In the Middle Ages, most local roads were mere tracks and therefore the old Roman Roads were generally used for long distance travel. Despite the fact that at the time being considered here these roads were already about a thousand years old, they were preferred by most travellers because, due to the Roman engineering techniques they had deeper foundations and much better drainage than the more recently developed roads which were basically simple tracks across the landscape.

It is perhaps significant that there were no Roman Roads through Sherwood Forest. The nearest Roman roads to the forest were the Fosse Way which runs in a north-easterly direction some five miles south-east of the edge of Sherwood Forest, and Ermine Street, also known at the time as Watling Street which runs in a south-easterly direction five miles north-east of the forest.

In the *Gest,* there is a claim that Robin built a church in Barnsdale dedicated to St Mary Magdalene. Campsall Church situated in Barnsdale, and only two or three miles from Wentdale is such a church and there is independent evidence that extensive building work was carried out on the church in the early fourteenth century. Although, there are many villages located in Sherwood Forest such as Edwinstowe, Clipstone, and Mansfield for example, none of these appear to be mentioned in the early ballads.

As described elsewhere the exploits for which Robin is most noted were waylaying travellers between York and London. The limestone ridge which runs from near Sunderland to Nottingham, passes through Barnsdale, but close to its eastern boundary. The Romans preferred to site their roads on high ground in order to avoid the often badly drained and marshy land on either side. The road currently known as Ermine Street ran along the crest of the limestone ridge, but just south of Doncaster, turned south-east at Bawtry, towards Lincoln. The Great North Road itself continued southwards towards Newark and London.

There was a major problem for the road builders in this part of England. The River Aire and the River Humber into which it flows were difficult to cross. The Romans located two sites where the rivers could be forded. One was at Castleford and the second twenty miles further east across the River Humber. At this point, near the present Humber Bridge, the river is one and a half miles wide and tidal. As described earlier, crossing here would be difficult and unreliable due to the tides although it would have been possible to use a ferry. Castleford is not located on the high ground of the limestone ridge, therefore to reach the ford at Castleford the road is diverted westwards at a point two and a half miles south of Wentbridge, known at the present time as Barnsdale Bar. It then descends from the ridge, and passes to the west of Thorp Marsh only half a mile from the village of Wentbridge.

It is recorded that William the Conqueror whilst on his way to put down a rebellion at York in 1069 was delayed for three weeks due to floods at the ford at Castleford. Many years earlier the Venerable Bede had recorded that after the battle of Winwoed many Mercian soldiers were drowned in the floods in 655. Some commentators consider that the name Winwoed applies to the river and have made many suggestions as to which river this might be, including the River Went, however there does not appear to be any evidence to support this view, and the only logical choice is the River Aire at Castleford.

Later a timber bridge was built but this would only have been wide enough to carry packhorses, the usual way of transporting goods at the time. However the river still caused problems for travellers as the approaches to the bridge had to cross the flood plain, which here is wide and the ground soft and marshy. As a result of coal mining operations in the nineteenth and twentieth centuries the area has been subject to extensive subsidence with the result that parts of the area have become permanently inundated and now form the Fairburn Ings Nature Reserve.

Historical and palynological records show that there were some particularly wet periods during the second part of the thirteenth and the early fourteenth centuries which would have rendered the crossing at Castleford more difficult than usual. At this time, in the absence of local authorities or other organisations responsible for the upkeep and possibly even the construction of the roads these duties were undertaken by the church. When Richard de Kellawe became Bishop of Durham in 1311, he offered indulgence of their sins to anyone who would provide money, materials or labour for the construction of a new causeway over Brotherton Marsh and a bridge over the river at Ferrybridge. The bridge consisted of six stone arches and included a chantry chapel. Not only did the chapel provide for a priest to say masses for the donors to the bridge but also for travellers who wished to pray for safe travel and it also no doubt served as a facility for the Church to collect the tolls or fees travellers had to pay for using the bridge.

Ferrybridge is situated four miles east of Castleford. Here the flood plain was narrower and the road could return to the higher ground much sooner. A new route was adopted along the ridge to rejoin the old Roman Road at Barnsdale Bar. It is likely that, as it is in reality a diversion around the difficult river crossing, it was also known as Watling Street in the Middle Ages. Significantly this new route was first brought into use in 1320, about the time Robin became an outlaw. Until 1963 when the Wentbridge Viaduct was constructed, this new road, known as the Great North Road, passed through Wentbridge village. If Robin decided that he had to resort to highway robbery, it would have been quite logical for him to move from Wakefield to Wentbridge which is on the new road, only half a mile from the old Roman road, and is only ten miles from Wakefield.

Further evidence of the local topography is available as shown on contemporary maps and although the Gough Map gives no indication of any main road through Sherwood Forest, there is in existence a detailed description of a journey made by the warden and fellows of Merton College in 1330AD from Oxford via Nottingham, Worksop and Mansfield to Doncaster. Two years later they repeated the journey but on this occasion passed through Ollerton rather than Mansfield. The fact that there were at least two and possibly more routes would have increased the difficulty for Robin in planning where to waylay any travellers. It also indicates that there was probably no direct main route through the forest.

An interesting feature of the Gough Map is the fact that it only shows four of the more than sixty royal forests in England namely: the Forest of Dean, Sherwood Forest, the New Forest and Inglewood Forest. Clearly Sherwood Forest was of major importance and much more widely known than Barnsdale in the fourteenth century, which is probably why the later fictitious embellishments to the Robin Hood story were described as happening there rather than in the lesser well-known Barnsdale. If the *Gest* was pure fiction, it is unlikely that Wentbridge, a rather obscure hamlet, would have been chosen as the earliest setting for the story in preference to the more widely known Sherwood Forest.

John Ogilby's map is dated 1698 and shows the details of the main route from London to Berwick by way of York. The part of the road in which we are interested is shown as passing through Stamford, Grantham, Newark, Tuxford, Doncaster, Wentbridge and Ferrybridge. It is interesting to note that apart from the section from Grantham to Bawtry, a distance of about forty miles out of a total two hundred miles, the route follows the old Roman road. Although the map refers to Sherwood Forest, it is shown passing five and a half miles east of Wellow, which at the time would have been only one and a half miles inside the forest boundary. At this point, which is the nearest the road comes to the forest boundary; it is still four miles from Sherwood Forest. By the time, Ogilby was producing his map Sherwood was of course no longer a royal forest with defined boundaries and the name had come to be applied to the area in general, as is presently the case with the Ordnance Survey map Sheet 270 Sherwood Forest.

Of the one hundred Ogilby maps only one shows a route passing through Sherwood Forest and this particular route runs from Oakham to Barnsley via Nottingham and Mansfield. It has to be remembered that this map dates from the very end of the seventeenth century, some 400 years after the time of Robin Hood's exploits.

It is interesting that despite the obvious importance of Nottingham and Sherwood Forest there is no indication on the Gough Map of any main road to either the city or through the forest. On the other hand, the Gough Map and others do show the former Roman Road called Ermine Street (also referred to at the time as Watling Street) running through Wentbridge and the centre of Barnsdale.

In the fourteenth century, the composition of the traffic using the roads would have been very diverse. Most of the travellers would have been pedestrians walking perhaps to the next village or to the nearest market town. Some may have been travelling much further; pilgrims perhaps. Other more wealthy individuals would of course be riding on horseback. In general, goods would have been carried by pack horses or mules, in trains of up to fifty animals with a trained lead horse at the head of the train. Other goods and passengers may have been carried in carts, some open, others with a canvass or other coarse material cover. Mostly these would be pulled by horses or in the case of about one in four by oxen because, although much slower than horses, oxen were better able to cope with difficult conditions and steeper gradients. Although during the Roman Empire, carts were generally fitted with brakes and were well sprung, by the fourteenth century such technology had completely fallen into disuse.

Unsprung carts and unpaved roads combined to ensure that travelling was both uncomfortable and very slow. In general, the maximum distance which could be travelled by a pedestrian would be about ten miles in a day and a cart would travel about twice as far. A person travelling on horseback would probably cover thirty miles in one day. Under certain circumstances these distances could possibly be doubled. It would be many years before stage coaches with a regular change of horses would be introduced. The limited daily travel distance meant that there was a demand for overnight en route accommodation which was provided by many roadside inns.

A major disadvantage from the point of view of travellers on any route running from north to south through Sherwood Forest is the fact that the first part of the journey from Ferrybridge southwards included traversing the full length of Barnsdale which was a well-known haunt of outlaws, possibly including Robin himself. As far as Robin Hood's activities are concerned, he may well have judged that all of the roads within Sherwood Forest lay within a few miles of Nottingham which was much too close to the home of the Sheriff of Nottingham for safety. The Gough Map shows the nearest Roman roads to Sherwood Forest are the road north from Derby to Chesterfield which at its nearest runs five miles west of the forest's western boundary and the Fosse way which is about two miles from its south eastern border. This route, like those through the forest is probably much too close to Nottingham itself for outlaws to operate in safety.

A more likely reason for Robin's decision to base his activities in Barnsdale is the fact that the travellers he intended to waylay, almost exclusively members of the clergy travelling south from York, would be using the Great North Road rather than taking the lengthy diversion through Sherwood. Travellers, if passing through Sherwood, would have been forced by the obstruction caused by the River Aire to have first passed through Barnsdale. Due to the well-known and recorded activities of the various outlaws operating in Barnsdale it is unlikely that by the time travellers reached Sherwood they would have retained sufficient funds to make robbery there worthwhile.

Robin's choice as to whether he should base his activities in Sherwood Forest or Barnsdale would probably have been based on tactical considerations. Map 2 shows various routes travellers could have taken between York and London superimposed on an extract from the Gough Map. The most obvious is that shown in a heavy red line whereas alternative routes are highlighted in a lighter line. The Gough Map itself shows no routes through Nottingham or Sherwood but the records of the Journeys of the Master and Fellows of Merton College indicate that at least two such routes were in use at the time. The fact that two different routes were used suggests that neither formed part of the main route from York to the south.

Travellers had the choice of three or four different routes at this point in their journey and as a result Robin would have three or four different options as to where he should prepare his ambush. The disadvantage of all of these locations is that whichever one the travellers chose, a few miles further north, as a result of the restrictions placed on them by the River Aire crossing, they would have had to pass through Doncaster and also cross the difficult valley of the River Went at Wentbridge.

It can be seen from photograph 9 that the sides of the valley are very steep and wooded and travellers going from North to South would have to descend the left-hand side of the valley before climbing the right-hand side. In medieval times, the more level ground on both sides would also have been thickly wooded making travelling even more dangerous and difficult.

In this connection, the *Gest* itself is absolutely clear. Sherwood is not mentioned at all whereas Barnsdale is mentioned no less than eight times.

'*Robyn stode in Bernesdale*'
Robin stood in Barnsdale.

However in another poem about Robin written about the same time as the *Gest* and called "Robin Hood and the Potter" the description of his whereabouts is even more specific:

Y met hem bot at Wentbreg,
seyde Lytyll John.
'I met them both at Wentbridge
said Little John'

There is further evidence in the *Gest* supporting the claim of Wentbridge, a village located at the centre of Barnsdale, to be the site of the action. It seems Robin's modus operandi was to stop travellers, offer them a meal and then make them pay for it, often with everything they were carrying. Stanzas 253 to 259 of the *Gest* describe how a monk travelling south to London was stopped, and after treating him to dinner Robin robbed him of all his possessions. On leaving, the monk complained that had he continued to Blyth or Doncaster his meal would have been cheaper. This episode indicates without doubt that the area where Robin was operating was a short distance north of Doncaster. Wentbridge is 11 miles north of Doncaster: the northern edge of Sherwood Forest is 21 miles south.

It is recorded that William de Lamberton, Bishop of St Andrews, Robert Wishart, Bishop of Glasgow, and Henry, Abbot of Scone, were captured in Scotland in 1306 and sent south to Winchester or Porchester. The route taken for part of the journey from Pontefract to Nottingham Castle was via Tickhill on the first day, via Newark on the second day and to Nottingham on the third day.

If they had followed the same route as the fellows of Merton College through Worksop and Mansfield to Nottingham, it would have shortened the journey by some twelve miles. Presumably there was a good reason for taking the longer route. Perhaps this route was chosen because the road was of a better standard or the castles at Tickhill and Newark offered more security. During the first part of the journey from Pontefract to Tickhill through Barnsdale their escort was increased to protect them from the outlaws known to be operating in the area. There does not appear to be any reference to the necessity for an escort for travellers in Sherwood Forest.

The topography of the Went Valley provides an ideal opportunity for waylaying travellers journeying south through Wentbridge. On the north side of the village, the track of the old medieval road descends at a slope of one in eight and then climbs out of the village on the south side at a slope of one in eleven. Both of these slopes would have hindered pedestrians and animals whichever way they were travelling. In addition, the road ran diagonally across the slope which has a straight gradient of one in five and is rough, rocky and overgrown. It would have provided adequate cover for an ambush.

Later in the seventeenth century it is recorded that the licensee of the Blue Bell Inn in Wentbridge had his license temporarily withdrawn because he had been harbouring "footpads and ne'er do wells". It was finally restored in 1633. This indicates that even three hundred years after Robin Hood, travellers through Barnsdale still risked being robbed. Obviously Wentbridge was a good spot for footpads to operate.

Also of course the *Gest* describes Robin's actions generally as being against people travelling south from York to London. Sixteen miles south of York is the River Aire which any travellers would have to cross at Ferrybridge or at the nearby Newton Abbey Ferry. From here, the route is south for the full length of Barnsdale through Wentbridge and Doncaster to Blyth. At Blyth, those travellers who had avoided the outlaws in Barnsdale would have to decide if they wanted to divert from what is known as the Great North Road to Worksop and Sherwood. The choice was not Barnsdale or Sherwood but having passed through Barnsdale, whether they should travel the extra distance and divert to Sherwood. Had Robin been in Sherwood he would not have been able to waylay travellers who had proceeded via the alternative route through Tuxford and Newark and had not travelled the extra ten miles through Sherwood.

In Camden's "Britannia", there is an account, possibly fictitious, which describes an incident involving Robin and the Bishop of Hereford. It is claimed that Robin, having robbed the bishop or holding him for ransom forced him to dance at a site beneath an oak tree in Skelbrooke Park which is just one mile south of Barnsdale Bar. The poem describing the incident makes it clear that it took place in Barnsdale and at least twenty miles from Sherwood.

At the time being considered here, Thomas the Earl of Lancaster called for men to join his rebellion against King Edward II. Robin Hode is not listed as failing to report for duty in the rebellion so it is assumed he was one of the rebels. On 16 March 1322, the Earl was defeated at the Battle of Boroughbridge and taken to Pontefract Castle, where he was held prisoner and was beheaded on 22 March. The rebels were outlawed and the records in Wakefield show a five-roomed house near the market was confiscated; perhaps this was Robert Hood's house.

It is assumed by many that Robin left the town and took refuge in the forest. Other rebels, named in the court records were John Nailer (Little John), W Schakelok (Will Scarlet) and Roger of Doncaster. Presumably they all fled with Robin to the forest although this may have been to avoid persecution for their religious convictions rather than to avoid retribution for supporting the rebels.

There is no mention in the *Gest* of Robin residing at either Nottingham or in Sherwood Forest although in all three ballads described below there is an account of him visiting Nottingham. The Sheriff of Nottingham is mentioned several times so it is assumed that this is the reason for the Nottingham connection. As Sherwood Forest and Barnsdale are only separated by about twenty miles and Sherwood Forest would have been better known, the later association with Sherwood was made. In "Robin Hood and the Monk", Robin declares his intention of going to Nottingham alone. Little John wants to go with him as it will be dangerous, but Robin tells him not to. The poem then says that Little John goes to Sherwood, part way to Nottingham. The clear implication is that Little John and Robin were not in Sherwood Forest on a regular basis, but were further north: no doubt in Barnsdale. After Robin leaves Nottingham, he is described as being in Sherwood but he would have had to pass through Sherwood Forest on his way back to Wentbridge and Barnsdale.

The significance of Conisbrough is that it is located north of Sherwood Forest and south of Barnsdale. It is clear that in returning to Barnsdale from Nottingham it would be necessary to pass through Sherwood Forest and then pass Conisbrough before reaching Wentbridge.

The situation regarding roads at the beginning of the fourteenth century was that the old Roman Road known at that time as Watling Street ran half a mile to the west of the village of Wentbridge and the Great North Road ran through the village. It is clear that these two main routes, the roads from the north of England and especially from York to London made Wentbridge and the valley of Wentdale an ideal place for Robin to base his operations.

At Wentbridge, the Great North Road has to cross the valley of the River Went, which has resulted in a very steep gradient, especially on the north side of the village. In 1830 or thereabouts, a new cutting was formed in the hillside using explosives and railway engineering techniques. This greatly reduced the slope but even so the gradient is still one in fourteen and on the section of the medieval road still visible the slope is considerably greater, estimated at one in eight. It does not take a great effort of the imagination to visualise the problems faced by a horse or ox drawn cart with only very rudimentary brakes or springs negotiating such a slope. Subsequently in 1963 the village was by-passed by the construction of a single span viaduct which crosses the entire valley.

At the southern end of the village is an area of high ground named on the current Ordnance Survey maps as Sayles Plantation which overlooks the Went Valley and the village of Wentbridge.

Take thy bowe in thy hande, sayde Robyn,
Late Much wende with the,
And so shal Wyllyam Scarlok,
And no man abyde with me,

And walke vp vnder the Sayles,
And to Watlynge-strete,
And wayte after some vnketh gest;
Vp-chaunce ye may them mete.
Take your good bow' said Robin
And let Much go with thee
And also take Will Scarlet,
And I will stay here.

And walk up under Sayles,
Then on to Watling Street,
And wait for some unknown guest;
In case one should pass by.

About half a mile south-east of Wentbridge village and forming part of the southern wall of the Went Valley, is an area of high ground known as the Sayles. It is well established that there are many references relating to the Sayles in historical records dating back to the thirteenth century and possibly earlier but the only recent information seems to be notes on the 1853 Ordnance Survey maps which show an area named as Sayles Plantation. The name does not appear on the 1840 OS maps nor on Jeffery's 1771 map of Yorkshire. The area was identified as Sayles Plantation by the historian Joseph Hunter in the nineteenth century but there is no indication of when the "Plantation" part of the name was first applied.

There appears to be some confusion about the description of the Sayles in the *Gest*. This is no doubt the result of the *Gest* relating two separate incidents and the misinterpretation of the Old English language used by the original composers. Adding to the confusion is the misconception of the physical shape of the valley and its surroundings.

The first incident described in the *Gest* recounts how Robin gave instructions to Little John to take Much the Miller's son and Will Scarlet to look out for travellers on the Great North Road. According to stanza 18 he told them:

And walke vp to the Saylis,
And so to Watlingr Strete,
And wayte after some unkuth gest,
Up chaunce ye may them mete.

But as they loked in to Bernysdale,
Bi a dern strete,
Than came a knyght ridinghe
Full sone they gan hym mete

And walk up to the Sayles
And so to Watling Street
And wait until some unknown stranger
You may possibly meet
But as they looked into Wentvale
By a hidden track,
A knight came riding;
Who they quickly went to meet.

It has generally been assumed that the top of Sayles affords a wide view over Wentbridge and Watling Street. To an extent this is correct but, resulting from the bend in the gorge-like valley the thickly wooded shoulder of the projecting valley side to the west almost completely obscures the view of Wentbridge and the road. This is clearly shown in the illustration (Photo 16). Even from the top of the Sayles the only part of Watling Street which would have been visible would be a stretch of a few hundred yards in the village itself and here of course travellers, even on horseback, would have been largely concealed by the buildings in the village. The Gest itself claims the track followed by the knight was hidden. Clearly as it descended the steep valley side, the road had broken into multiple tracks as described in Chapter 3 above.

The word "upstream" did not enter the English language until the late seventeenth century. The Old English format before that was to use the word "up" to describe the direction of flow of a stream or river. The first line in stanza 18 should therefore be regarded as an instruction to walk upstream to the Sayles rather than an instruction to climb the hill. To walk upstream to Sayles the starting point must obviously be downstream, for example in Brockadale, the ideal place for Robin and his men to have taken residence. When flying over Brockadale at low altitude, a number of markings were noticed on the flat valley floor which at this point is less than 100 yards wide. Whilst these markings may be due to flooding or other causes it would be interesting to carry out an aerial photographic or a geophysical survey to try and locate evidence of historic dwellings.

Having walked along the river bank to Sayles, Little John and his companions would have continued following the river until they came to the bridge in the centre of the village. Then they would have proceeded north and located the concealed track where they met the knight riding carefully down the very steep slope into the village. It is possible that the existing bridleway shown on photo 17 may in fact be the very track upon which the knight was travelling.

The second incidence referred to above is described in the section following stanzas 208 and 209 in the *Gest*. This is very similar to the previous reference to Wentbridge in so far as Robin directs his men to proceed to Watling Street to see if they can meet up with some travellers but the wording in the *Gest* is more explicit with reference to ascending Sayles. Stanza 209 reads:

And walke up under the Sayles,
And to Watlynge-strete,
And wayte after some unketh gest;
Up-chaunce ye may them mete,

And walk up under the Sayles
And to Watling Street

And wait for an unknown guest
You may perhaps meet.

The first two lines are clearly an instruction to walk upstream along the river bank, around the base of the Sayles, and then to continue along the river bank to Watling Street. There is obviously no intention that they should climb to the summit of Sayles.

Stanza 440 in the *Gest* tells of Robin's affection for Mary Magdalene.

I made a chapell in Bernysdale,
That semely is to se,
It is of Mary Magdaleyne,
And thereto wolde I be.

I built a chapel in Barnsdale
Which is pleasant to see
Dedicated to Mary Magdalene
And there I would like to be.

Churches dedicated to Mary Magdalene are not very common. There are only five within a twenty-mile radius of Wentbridge and three of these are modern. Of the remaining two churches, one is at Whiston near Rotherham and the second is in the village of Campsall. Whiston is approximately twenty miles from both Barnsdale and Sherwood, whereas Campsall is less than three miles from Wentdale and nearly forty from Sherwood. The architecture of some parts of the church is Norman so it was certainly in existence during the fourteenth century. As described above Pevsner claims extensive building work was being carried out on the church at Campsall in the late thirteenth and early fourteenth centuries. There is also a strong and persistent local legend that Robin was married at Campsall church. His wife was named Matilda, not Marian. Maid Marian only appears in one of the later poems, which were written during the reign of Henry VIII to add a little spice and entertainment value to the story.

Some commentators claim that the church referred to in the above stanzas from the *Gest* refer to the church at Skelbrooke, and that Barnsdale is centred on the shallow valley of the Skell but the church at Skelbrooke is dedicated to St

Michael & All Angels. Obviously, this cannot be the church referred to in the *Gest*.

There is also a church dedicated to St Mary Magdalene at Sutton in Ashfield in Sherwood Forest which obviously cannot be considered as being in Barnsdale, but the ballad claims that the church referred to is definitely located in Barnsdale.

There is possibly a further logistical reason for Robin to select Barnsdale rather than Sherwood Forest as a suitable area for his base. The ballads claim that his so-called merry men numbered up to 300 at various times and they also contain accounts of his men getting married. Presumably the wives and families of his men would also have been resident in the greenwood and together they would have formed a sizeable community. Providing food for such a large group could have presented a difficult problem, particularly during the period of the Great Famine. The widespread enclosure of lands had not commenced by the beginning of the fourteenth century which is the period we are examining here. The terrain in general would have consisted of wasteland, woodland, and commons with some large fields adjacent to villages used for pasture or subject to ridge and furrow cultivation.

As described above, Sherwood Forest and Barnsdale, although only about 40 miles apart, have very different types of soil. In Sherwood Forest, the soil, because it is derived from the underlying Keuper sandstone, tends to be dry and infertile which gives rise to a natural flora typical of heathland. The soil in Barnsdale is a blend of the sands and clays of the coal measures together with the hill wash from the limestone and tends to be much more productive, possibly an important consideration in view of the general effects of the famine and the apparent number of men and possibly their families who had to be provided for.

For Robin in exile, Wentdale just downstream from the village of Wentbridge would be an ideal location. As a result of the valley being formed in the limestone at the point where it overlies the more impermeable Ackworth Rock there are a number of springs which would have provided abundant supplies of fresh water. The valley sides being very steep, even precipitous in places, and probably thickly wooded compared with the sparse heathland flora of Sherwood, would have furnished ample cover and even facilitated defensive action if that was considered necessary.

Although there are no definite official records of Robin's whereabouts, there are one or two tantalising glimpses. The records of the court of Common Pleas show that in 1429 a judge stated:

'Robin Hood in Barnesdale Stood.'

To summarise there is no mention of Sherwood Forest in the *Gest*. The earliest reference linking Robin to Sherwood appears to be a much-quoted note in Manuscript 132 in the library of Lincoln Cathedral. The note, written in Latin, appears to have been written on a blank flysheet in a pre-existing manuscript, so it is impossible to date it. The note roughly translates as:

Robin Hood in Sherwood Stood.

As described earlier Robin Hood was a fairly common name so it is quite possible that the Robin referred to here is not necessarily the subject of the well-known legend. The manuscript itself is dated around 1421–1425 so the note was obviously written later than that, possibly up to one hundred years or more after Robin was active. Some commentators seem to accept this note as incontrovertible evidence that the location of Robin's activities was limited to Sherwood, whereas others point out that the writing was clearly the work of a schoolboy, whose writing and knowledge of Latin was somewhat limited, in which case the claim should be treated with a degree of caution.

1. L D Stamp, *Britain's Structure and Scenery* Collins (1948) p209
2. C J Holt, *Robin Hood,* Thames & Hudson Ltd. (2011) p93
3. D Baldwin, *Robin Hood,* Amberley Publishing Plc. (2011) p170

Chapter 7
The Religious Outlaw

Because the information we have about Robin Hood is so old and unreliable, almost every statement in an article about him should be qualified by the inclusion of either the word "possibly" or "probably". However, there can be no question about some of the claims made in previous chapters, because they are a matter of historical record. There is no doubt that in the early fourteenth century England was affected by the Great Famine, as a result of which many people died from malnutrition or starvation, although it might be reasonable to question whether the climate change which led to the famine was caused by the volcanic eruption in faraway New Zealand, although the eruption itself is a recorded fact.

Similarly, the fact that the country was struck by the Black Death which killed about a third of the survivors of the famine is undeniable. There is no doubt whatsoever that there was a church dedicated to St Mary Magdalene only two miles from Wentdale because it still exists and is still the active local parish church. Furthermore it would not make sense to question the claim by Sir Nikolaus Pevsner the eminent architectural historian, that extensive building work was carried out at the church in the late thirteenth and early fourteenth centuries. There are several other claims in the preceding chapters the validity of some of which may be questioned, but which, none the less, are supported by a considerable amount of reliable evidence.

Although, the facts concerning the landscape, locations and conditions have been well and reliably established, the facts surrounding Robin's life and actions are still shrouded in mystery. There are no historical records or eye witness reports. There are certainly historical and court records of people named "Robin Hood" but "Robin Hood" and its many variations were common names at the time, and there is no evidence that these records refer to "our" Robin Hood. The only information we have is contained in the numerous poems and ballads, most of which are not contemporary. Indeed it is known that much of the literature was not created until many, sometimes several hundred years, after the event. In a number of cases, the writings have been shown to be incorrect, for example in the case of the descriptions of locations, such as the Lancashire connection. Notwithstanding these factors it is necessary to rely on the poems and ballads for guidance. At best, the resulting descriptions can only be speculation.

The Merry Men.

The image many people have of Robin Hood and his "Merry Men" is of a highway robber and his gang of supporters who "robbed the rich and gave to the poor", but there does not appear to be any support for this idea in any of the early ballads. In the seventeenth and eighteenth century, it was very fashionable among the members of literary circles to revive old poems and ballads. Prominent among these writers was one Joseph Ritson, who was regarded at the time as somewhat unusual in that he was a vegetarian and launched many highly critical attacks on his fellow writers.

In 1795, he published a collection of ballads and poems about Robin Hood which included a brief essay giving his own ideas about the life of Robin Hood. This appears to be the first reference to the idea that Robin robbed the rich and gave to the poor. It is well known that Ritson was a supporter and admirer of the French revolution, the revolutionaries and their principles. He may well have been transplanting his own ideals onto Robin's character.

Holt's [1] comment on this aspect of the legend is interesting: *'But none of the extant ballads, early or late, presents the outlaws robbing a secular landlord; and none is concerned with robbing the rich, whether clerk or lay.*

Possibly the most surprising description of Robin Hood's Merry Men is given in the ballad entitled "Robin Hood and the Old Man".

(Robin put his horne to his mouth,
A loud blast cold he blow,
Full three hundred bold yeomen
Came raking all on a row.'

He put his horn to his mouth
And blew as hard as he could blow

At least three hundred bold yeomen
Came running in a line

Stanzas 229 and 230 of the *Gest* include the following words which paint a rather surprising picture of one hundred and forty men, wearing colourful striped cloaks and drawn up in a line like a company of soldiers on parade.

'Let blowe a horne,' sayd Robyn,
That felaushyp may vs knowe;
Seuen score of wyght yemen
Came pryckynge on a rowe
.

And euerych of them a good mantel
Of scarlet and of raye;
All they came to good Robyn,
To wyte what he wolde say.

They made the monke to wasshe and wype
And syt at his denere
Robyn Hode and Lytell Johan.
They served him both in-fere,

'Blow a horn,' said Robin,
That our fellowship may know.
And seven score of bold yeomen
Came riding in a row.

And each of them had a good cloak
Of scarlet with stripes;
They all came to Robin,
To learn what he had to say

They made the monk wash and dry,
And sit at his dinner,
Robin Hood and Little John
Both served him in company

An interesting point here is the use of the word fellowship when referring to a group of highway robbers; a point which is discussed below. It should also be noted that this part of the ballad does not describe Robin blowing his horn but giving directions for a horn (or horns) to be blown. It is likely that the large number of men involved would be well scattered and that a number of horns were blown in relays to cover a wide area of the forest.

It is well known that generally Robin's men wore uniforms of Lincoln Green, but there appears to be some discussion as to what colour this actually was. Lincoln Green was a term applied to a woollen material dyed with locally obtained vegetable dyes and was therefore relatively inexpensive, but a cloth dyed "greyne" was also produced at Lincoln and this cloth was coloured scarlet. Because the dyes used to dye this material had to be imported the material was much more expensive, possibly costing more than twice as much as the green material. As Robin and his men were living in the forest as outlaws for whatever reason, it is unlikely they would have favoured the brighter colours. At a time when, despite the cost differential most people favoured wearing mixed, brighter colours and occasionally even more expensive materials such as linen, silk and fur, Lincoln green, a deep olive-green colour, was not generally favoured except by the poorer members of society.

In fact, a group of merry men dressed in Lincoln green would have a similar appearance to a company of monks clad in their plain brown, black or white habits. This choice of colour and material would also have emphasised the fact that they eschewed a desire for earthly wealth. In view of the foregoing, the description in the *Gest* of the striped scarlet cloaks is rather surprising and may possibly be explained as "poet's licence".

It is difficult to consider Robin in isolation without his "Merry Men" but references to his men in the ballads create significant problems. First is the question of how many men were there? Stanzas four and five of the *Gest* name three: Will Scarlet, Much the Miller's son and Little John. However by stanza 229 this had increased to 140, a claim which is repeated in two later stanzas. Not only is this a surprisingly large number, it would probably equal or even exceed the entire adult male population of a village like Wentbridge, but they all appeared as a group and were all similarly attired when Robin blows his horn. In a later ballad, "Robin Hood and the Old Man" in which Robin rescues three men about to be executed, the number of men had increased to 300. This may well have been a temporary group assembled for the specific operation of rescuing the men about to be hanged.

According to the ballad "A True tale of Robin Hood" he was offered a pardon by the king on condition he surrendered. He considered accepting the offer but 100 of his men, on learning of the possibility of his surrendering, abandoned him leaving just 40. Yet another ballad explains that shortly before his death he only retained the allegiance of Little John. If, as has been suggested previously, Robin had contracted the plague it Is possible most of his men would have deserted him to avoid infection.

Although, there are problems dating many of the ballads, these latter two in particular create a difficulty as their earliest recorded dates appear to be during the seventeenth century and the king referred to is Richard I who reigned a century before the period being considered in this study.

Based on reports in some of the ballads it seems Robin's usual method of recruiting members for his fellowship of merry men was to pick a fight with travellers he met. After a while, he would then ask for quarter, blow his horn to summon his men and then ask his erstwhile opponent to join his band and offer him a regular payment and regular issues of clothing in Lincoln green. There does not appear to be any record, either before or after the new recruit had joined the fellowship of him receiving a share in the proceeds of any robbery or even the promise of such a share. In one of the early ballads however, it is claimed that Robin offered a new recruit an annual payment and clothing. If Robin had to provide a regular payment to his men, he probably obtained the necessary funding by stealing from the passing clergy.

The Famine.

As well as Robin's approach to life it is necessary to consider the general conditions prevailing at the time. The population of England at the time of the Norman Conquest has been estimated at approximately one million. In the subsequent three centuries, this had increased to three million. Initially due to the generally benign climate this presented no problems, although there were occasional crop failures and even local famines. By the beginning of the thirteenth century, however, the population had grown to such an extent that the land could only provide enough resources to support it under the best of conditions. There was no longer any margin for crop failures or even harvest shortfalls. At the same time however, the Western European climate was undergoing a slight change, with cooler and wetter summers, and earlier autumn storms. The climate had deteriorated to such an extent that the peasants in particular, who constituted some 95% of the population were beginning to suffer hunger and deprivation.

It is believed that the cataclysmic eruption of Mount Tarawera in New Zealand in 1315 completely changed the way of life for many years, not only in England, but in the whole of Europe. It has been suggested that the ash, carbon dioxide and sulphur dioxide cloud in the atmosphere which resulted from the eruption caused major climate changes. For possibly up to three years, there was prolonged and heavy rainfall and low temperatures. Not only did this cause problems with transport in marshy areas and areas susceptible to flooding, such as at the confluence of the Aire and Calder rivers described above, but it also caused severe crop failures. The ground became so sodden that seed which had already been planted failed to germinate due to the water-logged ground.

People were even forced to kill and eat some of their working and breeding animals and there were reports of parents abandoning their children and even reports of cannibalism in some parts of Europe. Crops were so poor that people had to eat whatever grain they had, so none was preserved for sowing the following year. This failure to preserve grain for propagation and the slaughter of the breeding stock resulted in the effects of the famine extending for several years, in fact until 1325. The overall result of this was to cause a huge increase in the cost of living and in the price of food in particular. This of course mainly affected the peasant subsistence farmers. It was only the rich who were able to lay in stocks of any food or other consumables for the following year, although even the wealthiest were later affected.

During the latter part of the thirteenth and the early fourteenth century, possibly as a result of the hardships encountered by the general population there was a substantial increase in the crime rate and a decline in morality throughout the country. Despite the draconian punishments inflicted on the perpetrators, poaching in the royal forests became very common. In fact, this was so widespread that during the king's trip in 1322–1323 he was so concerned at the decrease in the number of deer in the forests, and particularly at Plumpton Park near Knaresborough, that he ordered an investigation.

On his return to Nottingham, the king expressed a desire to meet Robin so as it was well-known that Robin would waylay high ranking churchmen, he was advised to disguise himself as an abbot. It is noticeable that he was not advised to appear as a wealthy merchant, presumably because Robin did not have a reputation for robbing anyone other than the clergy. The king did not take an army, just a few knights disguised as monks. There does not appear to be any mention in the ballads of Robin robbing anyone other than members of the clergy such as bishops and monks, although according to the ballad "A True *tale of Robin Hood"*, believed to have been written in the early seventeenth century, he does threaten to rob any rich miser who oppresses the poor.

According to stanza 377 of the *Gest,* when the king, disguised as an abbot, met Robin Hood a few miles south of Conisbrough Castle, Robin explained they had to take the king's deer because they had no other means of sustenance.

We be yemen of this foreste
Vnder the gren-wode tre;
We lyveby our kynges dere,
Other shyft have not wee.

We are yeomen of this forest
Under the greenwood tree
We live by our king's deer,
Other food we have not any.

People gathered what food they could from the forests: edible roots, plants, grasses, nuts and even bark from the trees. Although many people were badly weakened by malnutrition, initially relatively few appear to have died during 1315. The spring and summer of 1316 were cold and wet again and the population now had less energy and no food supplies in reserve. By the spring of 1317, all classes of society were suffering, although, as might be expected, the lower classes suffered the most. Many farm animals were slaughtered, draft animals were so weakened they could not pull a wagon or draw a plough, seed grain was eaten, young children were abandoned, and many of the old voluntarily stopped eating and died so that the younger members of the family might live to work the fields again. In general, it was assumed that the catastrophic weather conditions were the direct result of God's displeasure with the general sinfulness of the human race. A poem of the time (c 1320) reads:

When God saw that the world was so over proud

He sent a dearth on earth, and made it full hard,
A bushel of wheat was at four shillings or more,
Of which men might have had a quarter before...
And then they turned pale who had laughed so loud,
And they became all docile who before were so proud,
A man's heart might bleed for to hear the cry
Of poor men who called out, 'Alas! For hunger I die...'

The consequences of the Great Famine as this period came to be called were wide ranging. Previously the generally accepted truth was that all things were the result of God's actions and could be affected by the prayers of the Church and the Clergy. The continuance of the famine, its devastating effects and the complete failure of the prayers of the Church and the Papacy in particular to alleviate the situation, led to widespread disillusionment. The Church was very wealthy so the clergy, although affected, were to some extent protected from the worst effects of the famine. In addition some continued to exact fees, tithes and rent from the general population and of course to sell indulgences from the sins which they claimed were the reason God had inflicted the famine upon them. Robin's antagonism toward the organised Church is clearly demonstrated in stanza 15 of the *Gest* when he instructs Little John, Much, and Will Scarlet not to rob honest working people but:

These bishops and these archbishops,
You shall them beat and bind;

It must be remembered that these were also turbulent times. In addition to the hardships brought about by the severe famine and the outbreak of the Black Death in the early fourteenth century, excessive taxation to pay for the Hundred Years War and wage controls combined with escalating prices all led to general unrest which fomented the Peasants Revolt in 1381. Although this was only loosely connected to the religious protests, it is generally believed that many of the protesters were inspired by a radical priest called John Ball and his cry of:

When Adam delved and Eve span
Who was then the gentleman?

If Robin was the type of person described above, it is quite likely that he would have had great sympathy for the starving peasants, he may well have tried to ease their problems. If, as seems likely from some of the ballads, he was making regular payments to his men as well as providing their Lincoln green uniforms he would have found it necessary to obtain funding from somewhere and this would have been the passing clergy. Overall his actions would have resulted in relieving the Church of some of its wealth and returning it to the local economy.

As the church services, the bible and all the scriptural documents were in Latin and most of the population were in any case illiterate, they had to rely for all information and for instruction on Christian teaching on what they were told by the clergy.

It is often thought that the Bible was first translated into English under the direction of John Wycliffe during the last two decades of the fourteenth century. In fact, there were a number of partial translations before this. One of the best known is the Lindisfarne Gospels translated by the Provost of Chester-le-Street before the Norman Conquest. In most cases, the priest would read from one of the translations or relate a biblical story in English before proceeding with the formal service in Latin.

Also the populace could attend local performances of the mystery plays which were based on bible stories. Initially these too were performed in Latin but, as with the services, they would often be preceded by an introduction in English. Later the plays themselves would be performed in the vernacular.

The existence of these various translations and the teaching of religion in English tended to inspire dissent among certain members of the population, and possibly led to the creation and rise of the Lollard movement whose members rejected some of the teachings of the Catholic Church. Although it is not suggested that Robin Hood himself was a Lollard, it is possible that he espoused similar ideas. The Lollards were considered heretics by the Catholic Church and to a certain extent by the state. In 1410, only shortly after the time of Robin Hood's death, John Badby, a self-confessed Lollard, was burned to death for his heresy. The possibility has to be considered that Robin's twenty-two-year self-imposed existence as an outlaw in hiding in Wentdale was to avoid his being taken as a heretic or he may even have adopted some other transformation to conceal his true identity.

It is completely logical that any collection of like-minded individuals would have joined him from quite a wide area, which would explain his unusually large number of followers. It is easy to accept that such a group would assemble based on their religious convictions rather than on a desire to share in the proceeds of highway robbery.

It is a remarkable coincidence that at this time, when Robin Hood was apparently relatively inactive and taking refuge in the greenwood there were in England two other men who in contrast were very active. It is even more remarkable that both these characters shared the same Christian name, 'Richard' and according to the information which is currently available both were born close to the year 1290.

Although they shared a Christian name, their identities were separated by their surnames. Richard Rolle was born in Thornton le Dale in North Yorkshire, although he was not a member of the clergy, he was educated at Oxford University and was a prolific writer on secular and religious matters. Initially his writings were in Latin but he later wrote in English. He died, probably as a result of the plague, in 1349, around the time of Robin's possible death. Later in life he adopted a hermit's lifestyle living at or close to a minor priory at Hampole near Doncaster. At this time, he became better known as Richard Rolle of Hampole. The other Richard chose to use either his birthplace or the name of the village where he lived and was known as Richard at Campsall.

It is shown above that the church which Robin Hood claimed to have built was also at Campsall and he ambushed travellers on the Great North Road at Wentbridge. A further coincidence becomes obvious when considering the location of the various villages mentioned above.

The road junction on the great North Road known as Barnsdale Bar serves as a useful reference point. The locations concerned, including Wentbridge, Campsall, Hampole, as well as Brockadale and the author's home at Upton all lie within two and a half miles of Barnsdale Bar: a fairly compact area.

In the thirteenth century, it was rather uncommon for individuals, particularly country individuals to attend university, but apparently both Richard Rolle and Richard Campsall studied at the same college at Oxford. It is known that Richard Campsall had received a Master of Arts qualification in theology around 1308 but there is no record at all of Richard Rolle qualifying. This has led to speculation that he felt dissatisfied with the contents of his studies and had left the university before the end of his course. It is inconceivable that two such characters whose lives followed such close parallel courses and were domiciled within less than three and a half miles of each other apparently did not come into contact with each other.

However there is possibly another completely different scenario. Suppose Richard Rolle and Richard Campsall were one and the same person using different names at different stages in his life. He could have used the name Richard Rolle when he was referring to the time he was preaching or writing, and Richard Campsall in any connections with the University. Clearly this explains why there is no record at the University of Richard Rolle obtaining any qualifications.

This distinction applied even after his death because he died, probably as a result of the plague, as Richard Rolle on 30 September 1349 at Hampole but was later buried in the choir at Merton College Chapel in Oxford as Richard Campsall.

If he occasionally wanted to remain incognito for example when acquiring some of the churches property or humiliating members of the clergy or appearing in court, he made his life even more complicated by adopting the universal alias Robin Hood.

The early years of Rolle's life appear to be fairly well documented, as are his later years when he lived as a hermit at Hampole but there does not appear to be a detailed record of his activities in the interim period. It is suggested that he spent this time travelling between various religious establishments writing and preaching. It is significant that this period appears to be between the dates of 1322 and 1349. Whereas the time Robin spent in the greenwood as calculated above lies between 1324 and 1349.

Robin's life on the other hand is recorded in the ballads as a series of isolated incidents, none of which exclude the possibility that they are actually one and the same person, and that "Robin Hood" was in fact Richard Rolle's alias which he used when attacking the established church.

Although this idea may initially seem rather bizarre, further consideration reveals that it is in reality quite logical. In chapter 1 above, it is claimed that references to the name "Robin Hood" extend over a period exceeding 150 years and are fairly widespread over the whole country. These references occur not only in ballads but also, and more significantly, in official court records. This has led a number of authors and historians to conclude that the name "Robin

Hood" was in effect a form of generic alias. If Richard Rolle was seeking an alter ego in these circumstances, Robin Hood would have been an obvious choice.

A further point which deserves some attention is the fact that a very close relationship had developed between Robin and Sir Richard at the Lee, the future Earl of Arundel. This would have been much more likely to have occurred between Richard Rolle and a mere yeoman farmer.

Stanza 450 of the *Gest* explains that after serving the king for about a year Robin spent twenty-two and a half years in the greenwood. The *Gest* does not explain what he did during that lengthy period. However, the mystery is completely cleared if the suggestion that Robin Hood and Richard Rolle was one and the same person is correct.

It is interesting to re-examine the general conditions prevailing in the locality at the time. There is clear evidence that valuable merchandise and personnel travelling along the Great North Road had an augmented escort. This would of course have necessitated a corresponding increase in the number of Robin's men to guarantee a successful heist.

It is difficult to visualise a group of so-called outlaws living in the greenwood at this time, as it coincided with the early years of the Great Famine, and although the extreme rainfall experienced during the years immediately following the New Zealand volcanic eruption in 1315 would have eased the rainfall would probably have still remained excessive.

The life-threatening shortages caused by the famine demanded that the attention of the local residents was fully focussed on easing the resulting problems. This meant that instead of living as a group in the greenwood, as often supposed, they remained at their homes, pursuing their normal occupations whilst awaiting a rallying horn signal before proceeding at speed to Brockadale and hence to "Watling Street" at Wentbridge.

The question which arises here is, 'What was Robin himself doing during this period?' He had adopted his alter ego, Richard Rolle, and was either travelling the local area teaching and preaching, or was in residence at Hampole Priory.

It is appreciated that the foregoing evidence that Robin Hood and Richard Rolle are one and the same person is possibly circumstantial but it is none the less evidence and more substantial than that contained in most of the other literature on the subject.

Hampole, Robin's adopted place of residence was a very small hamlet or village which did not have a church although Campsall, located only three and a half miles away was a much larger village or even a small town and possessed an elegant Norman church which according to the *Gest* Robin claimed to have built.

As mentioned above Robin had, and still has, a reputation for robbing the rich and giving to the poor. But unlike other matters discussed previously there does not appear to be any hard evidence concerning this aspect of his life and there is no mention in the *Gest* apart from the last stanza:

Cryst haue mercy on his soule,
That dyed on the rode!
For he was a good outlawe,
And dyde pore men moch god.

Christ have mercy on his soul,
Who died on the Cross.
For he was a good outlaw,
And did poor men much good.

It is of course possible to do poor men much good without necessarily giving gifts of money. Several of the ballads describe Robin and his men rescuing individuals who are being held prisoner, in some cases awaiting execution, for crimes such as poaching deer and other game from the royal parks and forests.

In the seventeenth century a poet, Martin Parker, wrote a poem entitled "A true tale of Robin Hood" which contains the following stanza:

With wealth which he by robbery got
Eight almes-houses he built.
Thinking thereby to purge the blot
Of blood which he had spilt.

It is claimed that it is based on an earlier black-letter copy, but it is impossible to verify or date this except to say black-letter documents were introduced after about 1150. Unfortunately it has not been possible to locate the almshouses described in the poem.

The ballad "Robin Hood and the Tinker" includes a description of Robin giving the tinker one hundred pounds, but this appears to be the tinker's fee for joining Robin's band, and represents his first year's pay and cannot therefore be regarded as an outright gift. The only record of such a gift appears in the rather later ballad "Robin Hood and the Bishop" in which an old woman claims when talking to Robin:

For I remember one Saturday night,
Thou brought me both shoes and hose;
Therefore I'le provide thy person to hide,
And keep thee from thy foes.

However, it may be that an investigation of the nature of the man himself, together with the conditions existing in England at the time, could shed some light on the subject. He was obviously a complex character as evidenced by the fact that after he had been pardoned by the king he voluntarily went into exile in the "green wood" for over twenty years, and presumably adopted a lifestyle similar to that of a hermit.

As mentioned above there are several records in the Wakefield Court Rolls of a person named Robin Hood appearing in court for various reasons. One record that is of particular interest is the claim that he was fined for failing to attend a muster of men to fight the Scottish invaders, presumably at the battle of Myton, fought on 20 September 1319.

A little time later there is a record of another hearing concerning a muster of men to support the Earl of Lancaster in his campaign against King Edward II. Robin Hood does not appear among those who failed to attend. This may be due to the fact that he was not among those selected to attend, but is more likely due to the fact that he did attend the muster and fought with the Earl at the Battle of Boroughbridge on 16 March 1322. The Lancastrian troops were hopelessly routed and outmanoeuvred and finally defeated. The Earl himself was captured, taken to Pontefract Castle, tried and beheaded on 22 March. Robin Hood may also have been captured, tried and outlawed for his part in the rebellion, or possibly that in order to avoid capture he voluntarily became an outlaw in the wooded area known as Barnsdale, just six miles south of Pontefract. In either case, he cannot be regarded as a common criminal, but more as a political outlaw. The fact that he supported the Earl of Lancaster in his action against the idle and ineffectual king does not preclude him feeling sympathy, and taking action to assist the poor. It is clear from the *Gest* that he was devoted to St Mary Magdalene and as a devout Christian he may well have felt it incumbent on himself to aid and give alms to the poor, if only to guarantee his own redemption.

When considering this aspect of the story, it is essential firstly to establish who were the rich and who were the poor. Many commentators, especially film and television producers, have assumed that the Saxon peasants were cruelly oppressed by the Norman invaders. However the period under consideration is some three hundred years after the Conquest and the Normans had to a certain extent been absorbed by the Saxons. English had become the language in everyday use and also in literature, by Chaucer for example, and both the French and Norman-French languages had to a large extent fallen out of use. Latin, of course was still used for legal and ecclesiastical purposes. The postulation that Robin supported the Saxons who were oppressed by the Norman invaders appears to date back to the publication of the novel Ivanhoe by Walter Scott in 1820.

It is admitted that after the Conquest William the Conqueror had seized many of the previously Saxon-owned estates and distributed them to the Norman nobles who had supported him. The anglicising process had been assisted by the fact that women were able to own property and as a result of the turbulent times there were a considerable number of wealthy widows so intermarriage between Norman and Saxon was not uncommon. Despite the blending of Saxon and Norman, the larger estates were still held by barons of Norman extraction and many who also still held estates in France.

The large number of merry men as described above presents a problem when considering Robin's activities as a highway robber. It is difficult to visualise a large group of basically criminals acting in unison without breaking into smaller sections, disputing the distribution of the proceeds of their crimes and apparently taking orders from any one individual. One of the principles when organising a criminal gang is to keep the numbers to a minimum, consistent with efficiency and security, in order to maximise the individual profit when sharing the proceeds.

Comparing Robin's supposed thefts with more recent events in England, it seems the large number of his supporters would have proved a liability rather than an asset. There were only fourteen members of the gang who carried out the Great Train Robbery in 1963 and shared £49.6m at present day (2015) values.

Fourteen were the minimum required because it was necessary to have people with knowledge of postal work, railway operations, including scheduling and signalling and importantly they needed someone who could drive a train. During Easter 2015 a gang of nine men carried out a raid on the Hatton Garden Safe Deposit Ltd. broke into the strong room and stole the contents of seventy safety deposit boxes. Both these raids were complex, required a great amount of planning and a number of expert technicians. By comparison, Robin's raids only required enough men in ambush to frighten off or defeat any possible escort and capture a cart full of treasure. It seems likely there was some reason other than greed or even the desperation resulting from the famine for so many men to join his outlaw band.

The problems which become apparent when considering the functioning of a large band of highway robbers suggest that there may be some reason other than outright avarice for the group to form and to show allegiance to Robin for many years. It may help in determining that reason to examine Robin's lifestyle and way of thinking. His most obvious preoccupation is an intense dislike for the Catholic Church. There are many instances described in the ballads of him robbing clergymen of all ranks but very few, if any, reports of him robbing anyone not directly connected to the church. In the earliest stanzas of the *Gest*, he is quoted as instructing his first men not to rob honest workers but to "beat and bind bishops and archbishops".

Despite his intense dislike of the church, he is obviously a devoted Christian and is particularly devoted to Saint Mary Magdalene, a point emphasised in the *Gest* where it is claimed he made a chapel dedicated to her in Barnsdale.

There is of course a more prosaic explanation of his apparent generosity. If, as an outlaw he was being hunted by the authorities, although this seems unlikely following his pardon, he would have possibly found it necessary to purchase the silence of those about him. Also if the proceeds of his highway robbery were reasonably high, he would have had to find some means of disposing of his wealth.

1. C J Holt, *Robin Hood* Thames and Hudson (2011) p37

THE GEST OF ROBIN HOOD

by: Stephen Knight (Editor), Thomas H. Ohlgren (Editor)
from: Robin Hood and Other Outlaw Tales 1997

The First Fytte
1 Lythe and listin, gentilmen, (Come)
That be of frebore blode; (Freeborn)
I shall you tel of a gode yeman, (yeoman)
His name was Robyn Hode.

2 Robyn was a prude outlaw, (proud)
Whyles he walked on grounde;
So curteyse an outlawe as he was one (courteous)
Was never non founde.

3 Robyn stode in Bernesdale,
And lenyd hym to a tre; (leaned against a tree)
And bi hym stode Litell Johnn,
A gode yeman was he. (Yeoman)

4 And also dyd gode Scarlok,
And Much, the miller's son;
There was none ynch of his bodi (inch)
But it was worth a grome. (whole man)

5 Than bespake Lytell Johnn
All untoo Robyn Hode: (unto)
Maister, and ye wolde dyne betyme (dine soon)
It wolde doo you moche gode. (much good)

6 Than bespake hym gode Robyn:
To dyne have I noo lust, (hunger)
Till that I have som bolde baron,
Or som unkouth gest. (unknown guest)

7 That may pay for the best,
Or som knyght or squyer, (knight or squire)
That dwelleth here bi west.

8 A gode maner than had Robyn; (custom)
In londe where that he were,
Every day or he wold dyne (before he would dine)
Thre messis wolde he here. (masses he would hear)

9 The one in the worship of the Fader,
And another of the Holy Gost,
The thirde of Our der Lady,
That he loved allther moste. (most of all)

10 Robyn loved Oure der Lady;
For dout of dydly synne, (fear of deadly sin)
Wolde he never do compani harme
That any woman was in.
11 'Maistar,' than sayde Lytil Johnn,
'And we our borde shal sprede, (If; table)
Tell us wheder that we shal go, (where)
And what life that we shall lede.'

12 'Where we shall take, where we shall leve,'
Where we shall abide behynde;
Where we shall robbe, where we shal reve, (plunder)
Where we shal bete and bynde. (beat and tie up)

13 'Therof no force,' than sayde Robyn;
'We shall do well inowe; (enough)
But loke ye do no husbonde harme, (peasant farmer)
That tilleth with his ploughe.'

14 'No more ye shall no gode yeman (yeoman)
That walketh by grene-wode shawe;(thicket)
Ne no knyght ne no squyer

That wol be a gode felawe.'

15 'These bisshoppes and these archebishoppes,
Ye shall them bete and bynde;
The hy sherif of Notyingham,
Hym holde ye in your mynde.'

16 'This worde shalbe holde,' sayde Lytell Johnn, (kept)
'And this lesson we shall lere;
It is fer days God sende us a gest, (the day is far gone)
That we were at oure dynere!' (our dinner)

17 'Take thy gode bowe in thy honde,' sayde Robyn;
'Late Much wende with the;   (Let; go)
And so shal Willyam Scarlok,
And no man abyde with me. (Stay)'

18 'And walke up to the Saylis,
And so to Watlingr Strete,

And wayte after some unkuth gest, (unknown)
Up chaunce ye may them mete. (By chance)'

19 'Be he erle, or ani baron,
Abbot, or ani knyght,
Bringhe hym to lodge to me; (meet)
His dyner shall be dight.'(Ready)

20 They wente up to the Saylis,
These yeman all thre;
They loked est, they loked weest;
They myght no man see.

21 But as they loked in to Bernysdale,
Bi a dern strete, (concealed)
Than came a knyght ridinghe;

Full sone they gan hym mete. (They met him at once)

22 All dreri was his semblaunce, (dreary)
And lytell was his pryde;
His one fote in the styrop stode, (stirrup)
That othere wauyd beside.

23 His hode hanged in his iyn two;   eyes
He rode in symple aray;
A soriar man than he was one (more sorry)
Rode never in somer day.

24 Litell Johnn was full curteyes, (courteous)
And sette hym on his kne: (knelt)

'Welcom be ye, gentyll knyght,
Welcom ar ye to me.'

25 'Welcom be thou to grene wode, (the greenwood)
Hend knyght and fre;
My maister hath abiden you fastinge, (waited for you)
Syr, al these ouris thre.' (three hours)

26 'Who is thy maister?' sayde the knyght;
Johnn sayde, Robyn Hode;
'He is gode yoman,' sayde the knyght,
'Of hym have I herde moche gode. (Much good)'

27 'I graunte,' he sayde, 'with you to wende,
My bretherne, all in fere;
My purpos was to have dyned to day
At Blith or Dancastere.'

28 Furth than went this gentyl knight,
With a carefull chere; (worried expression)
The teris oute of his iyen ran, (tears ran from his eyes)

And fell downe by his lere (face)

29 They brought hym to the lodge door;
Whan Robyn hym gan see,
Full curtesly dyd of his hode (took off his hood)
And sette hym on his knee. (knelt down)

30 'Welcome, sir knight,' than sayde Robyn,
'Welcome art thou to me;

I have abyden you fastinge, sir, (waited)
All these ouris thre.' (three hours)

31 Than answered the gentyll knight,
With word s fayre and fre;
God the save, goode Robyn,
And all thy fayre meyné. (men)

32 They wasshed togeder and wyped bothe
(washed anddried their hands together)
And sette to theyr dynere;
Brede and wyne they had right ynoughe, (enough)
And noumbles of the dere. (Offal)

33 Swannes and fessauntes they had full gode,
And foules of the ryvere; (birds; river)
There fayled none so litell a birde (They lacked)
That ever was bred on bryre. (Branch)

34 'Do gladly, sir knight,' sayde Robyn;
'Gramarcy, sir,' sayde he; (Grant mercy (thank you))
'Suche a dinere had I nat
Of all these wekys thre. (weeks)'

35 'If I come ageyne, Robyn,
Here by thys contre,

As gode a dyner I shall the make (thee)
As that thou haest made to me.'

36 'Gramarcy, knyght,' sayde Robyn;
'My dyner whan that I it have,
I was never so gredy, bi dere worthy God, (hungry.)
My dyner for to crave.'

37 'But pay or ye wende,' sayde Robyn; (before you leave)
'Me thynketh it is gode ryght;
It was never the maner, by dere worthi God,   (custom)
A yoman to pay for a knyhht.'

38 'I have nought in my coffers,' saide the knyght,
'That I may profer for shame:'
'Litell Johnn, go loke,' sayde Robyn,
'Ne let nat for no blame.'

39 'Tel me truth,' than saide Robyn,
'So God have parte of the:' (protect)
'I have no more but ten shelynges,' sayde the knyght,
'So God have parte of me.'

40 If thou hast no more,' sayde Robyn,
'I woll nat one peny;
And yf thou have nede of any more,
More shall I lend the.'

41 'Go nowe furth, Littell Johnn,
The truth tell thou me;
If there be no more but ten shelinges, (shillings)
No peny that I se.'

42 Lyttell Johnn sprede downe hys mantell
Full fayre upon the grounde,
And there he fonde in the knyght s cofer

But even halfe pounde. (1pound = 20 shillings)

43 Littell Johnn let it lye full styll, (undisturbed)
And went to hys maysteer lowe;
'What tidyng s, Johnn?' sayde Robyn;
'Sir, the knyght is true inowe.'(enough)

44 'Fyll of the best wine,' sayde Robyn,
'The knyght shall begynne;
Moche wonder thinketh me (Much)
Thy clothynge is so thin.'

45 'Tell me one worde,' sayde Robyn,
'And counsel shal it be;
I trowe thou warte made a knyght of force,
Or ellys of yemanry. (else)'

46 'Or ellys thou hast bene a sori husbande, (poor)
And lyved in stroke and stryfe; (lived)
An okerer, or ellis a lechoure,' sayde Robyn,(usurer or lecher)
'Wyth wronge hast led thy lyfe.'

47 'I am none of those,' sayde the knyght,
'By God that mad me;
An hundred wynter here before
Myn auncetres knyghtes have be. (ancestors knights)'

48 'But oft it hath befal, Robyn,
A man hath be disgrate; (discredited)
But God that sitteth in heven above
May amende his state.'

49 'Withyn this two yere, Robyne,' he sayde,
'My neghbours well it knowe, (knew it well)
Foure hundred pounde of gode money
Ful well than myght I spende.'

50 'Nowe have I no gode,' saide the knyght, (possessions)
'God hath shaped such an ende,
But my chyldren and my wyfe,
Tyll God yt may amende.'

51 'In what maner,' than sayde Robyn,
'Hast thou lorne thy rychesse?' (lost, riches)
'For my great foly,' he sayde,
'And for my kyndnesse.'

52 'I hade a sone, forsoth, Robyn,
That shulde have ben myn ayre, (heir)
Whanne he was twenty wynter olde,
In felde wolde iust full fayre. (Joust)'

53 'He slewe a knyght of Lancaster,
And a squyer bolde;
For to save hym in his ryght
My godes both sette and solde. (goods, pledged)'

54 'My londes both sette to wedde, Robyn, (security
untyll a certayn day,)
To a ryche abbot here besyde
Of Seynt Mari Abbey.' (Saint Mary's)

55 'What is the som?' sayde Robyn;
'Trouth than tell thou me;'
'Sir,' he sayde, 'Foure hundred pounde;
The abbot told it to me.' (counted it out)

56 'Nowe and thou lese thy lond,' sayde Robyn, (lose)
'What woll fall of the?'
'Hastely I wol me buske,' sayd the knyght, (hasten)
'Over the salt see,'
57 'And se where Criste was quyke and dede, (alive)
On the mount of Calver (Calvary)

Fare wel, frende, and have gode day;
It may no better be.'

58 Teris fell out of hys iyen two; (eyes)
He wolde have gone hys way:
'Farewel, frende, and have gode day;
I ne have no more to pay.'

59 'Where be thy frend s?' sayde Robyn:
'Syr, never one wol me knowe;
While I was ryche ynowe at home
Great boste than wolde they blowe. (boast, spread)'
60 'And nowe they renne away fro me, (run)
As bestis on a rowe;
They take no more hede of me (notice)
Thanne they had me never sawe.'
61 For ruthe thanne wept Litell Johnn, (pity)
Scarlok and Muche in fere; (together)
'Fyl of the best wyne,' sayde Robyn,
'For here is a symple chere. (friendship)'

62 'Hast thou any frende,' sayde Robyn,
'Thy borowe that wold be?' (security)
'I have none,' than sayde the knyght,
'But God that dyed on tree.'

63 'Do away thy iapis,' than sayde Robyn, (jokes)
'Thereof wol I right none;

    Wenest thou I wolde have God to borowe, (Do you think)
Peter, Poule, or Johnn?'

64 'Nay, by hym that me made,
And shope both sonne and mone,
Fynde me a better borowe,' sayde Robyn,
'Or money getest thou none.'

65 'I have none other,' sayde the knyght,
'The sothe for to say, (truth)
But yf yt be Our der Lady; (if it)
She fayled me never or thys day.'

66 'By dere worthy God,' sayde Robyn,
'To seche all Englonde thorowe,
Yet fonde I never to my pay (satisfaction)
A moche better borowe. (Security)'

67 'Come nowe furth, Litell Johnn,
And go to my tresouré
And bringe me foure hundered pound,
And loke well tolde it be.' (counted)

68 Furth than went Litell Johnn,
And Scarlok went before;
He tolde oute foure hundred pounde
By eight and twenty score.

69 'Is thys well tolde?' sayde litell Much;
Johnn sayde, 'What greveth the?
It is almus to helpe a gentyll knyght, (alms)
That is fal in poverté (poverty)'

70 'Master,' than sayde Lityll John,
'His clothinge is full thynne;
Ye must gyve the knight a lyveray, (livery (outfit))
To lappe his body therin. (clothe)'

71 'For ye have scarlet and grene, mayster,
And many a riche aray;
Ther is no marchaunt in mery Englond
So ryche, I dare well say.'
72 'Take hym thre yerdes of every colour, (Give)
And loke well mete that it be;' (measured)

Lytell Johnn toke none other mesure
But his bow-tree.

73 And at every handfull that he met
He leped foots three; (added)
'What devyll s drapar,' sayid litell Muche,
'Thynkest thou for to be?'

74 Scarlok stode full stil and loughe, (laughed)
And sayd, By God Almyght,
Johnn may gyve hym gode mesure,
For it costeth hym but lyght. (Little)

75 'Mayster,' than said Litell Johnn
To gentill Robyn Hode,
'Ye must give the knight a hors,
To lede home this gode.' (carry, gear)

76 'Take hym a gray coursar,' sayde Robyn, (fast saddle horse)
'And a saydle newe;
He is Oure Ladye's messangere;
God graunt that he be true.'

77 'And a gode palfray,' sayde lytell Much,
(smaller horse)
'To mayntene hym in his right;'

'And a peyre of botes,' sayde Scarlock,
'For he is a gentyll knight.'

78 'What shalt thou gyve hym, Litell John?' said Robyn;
'Sir, a peyre of gilt sporis clene, (spurs)
To pray for all this company;
God bringe hym out of tene.' (Misery)

79 'Whan shal mi day be,' said the knight, (repayment day)

'Sir, and your wyll be?'
'This day twelve moneth,' saide Robyn,
'under this grene-wode tre.'

80 'It were greate shame,' sayde Robyn,
'A knight alone to ryde,
Without squyre, yoman, or page,
To walk by his syde.'

81 'I shall the lende Litell John, my man,
For he shal be thy knave; (servant)
In a yeman's stede he may the stande, (place, serve)
If thou greate ned have.'

The Seconde Fytte

82 Now is the knight gone on his way;
This game hym thought full gode;
Whanne he loked on Bernesdale
He blessyd Robyn Hode.

83 And whanne he thought on Bernysdale,
On Scarlok, Much, and Johnn,
He blyssyd them for the best company
That ever he in come.

84 Then spake that gentyll knyght,
To Lytel Johan gan he saye,
To-morrowe I must to Yorke toune,
To Saynt Mary abbay.

85 And to the abbot of that place
Foure hondred pounde I must pay;
And but I be there upon this nyght
My londe is lost for ay. (Forever)

86 The abbot sayd to his covent, (convent (of monks))
There he stode on grounde,
This day twelfe moneth came there a knyght
And borowed foure hondred pounde.

87 He borowed foure hondred pounde,
Upon all his lond fre;
But he come this ylk day (Unless)
Dysheryte shall he be. (Disinherited)

88 'It is full erely,' sayd the pryoure, (prior)
'The day is not yet ferre gone; (far)
I had lever to pay an hondred pounde,
And lay downe anone.'

89 'The knyght is ferre beyonde the see,
In Englonde is his ryght,
And suffreth honger and colde,
And many a sory nyght.'

90 'It were grete pyté' said the pryoure,
'So to have his londe;
And ye be so lyght of your consyence, (untroubled by)
Ye do to hym moch wronge.'

91 'Thou arte ever in my berde,' sayd the abbot,
'By God and Saynt Rycharde;'
With that cam in a fat-heded monke,
The heygh selerer. (high cellarer)

92 'He is dede or hanged,' sayd the monke,
'By God that bought me dere,
And we shall have to spende in this place
Foure hondred pounde by yere.'

93 The abbot and the hy selerer
Sterte forthe full bolde,
The hye iustyce of Englonde
The abbot there dyde holde.

94 The hye iustyce and many mo
Had take in to theyr honde
Holy all the knyght s det, (debt)
To put that knyght to wronge.

95 They demed the knyght wonder sore, (severly judged)
The abbot and his meyné: (men)
'But he come this ylk day (Unless, same)
Dysheryte shall he be.'

96 'He wyll not come yet,' sayd the iustyce,
'I dare well undertake;'
But in sorowe tym for them all (a bad time)
The knyght came to the gate.

97 Than bespake that gentyll knyght
Untyll his meyné:
Now put on your symple wedes (clothes)
That ye brought fro the see.

98 They put on their symple wedes,
They came to the gates anone;
The porter was redy hymselfe,
And welcomed them everychone. (Everyone)

99 'Welcome, syr knyght,' sayd the porter;
'My lorde to mete is he, (at dinner)
And so is many a gentyll man,
For the love of the.'

100 The porter swore a full grete othe,
By God that mad me,
Here be the best coresed hors (bodied)
That ever yet sawe I me.

101 'Lede them in to the stable,' he sayd,
'That eased myght they be;'
'They shall not come therin,' sayd the knyght,
'By God that dyed on a tre.'

102 Lorde's were to mete isette (seated at dinner)
In that abbotes hall;
The knyght went forth and kneled downe,
And salued them grete and small. (Saluted)

103 'Do gladly, syr abbot,' sayd the knyght,
'I am come to holde my day:'
The fyrst word the abbot spake,
'Hast thou brought my pay?'

104 'Not one peny,' sayd the knyght,
'By God that maked me;'
'Thou art a shrewed dettour,' sayd the abbot;
(crafty debtor)
'Syr iustyce, drynke to me.'

105 'What doost thou here,' sayd the abbot,
'But thou haddest brought thy pay' (Unless)
'For God,' than sayd the knyght,
'To pray of a lenger daye.' (beg, more time)

106 'Thy daye is broke,' sayd the iustyce,
(You are too late)
'Londe getest thou none:'
'Now, good syr iustyce, be my frende,
And fende me of my fone!' (defend, foes)

107 'I am holde with the abbot,' sayd the iustyce,
'Both with cloth and fee:'
'Now, good syr sheryf, be my frende!'
'Nay, for God,' sayd he.

108 'Now, good syr abbot, be my frende,
For thy curteys
And holde my lond s in thy honde
Tyll I have made the gree! (Paid the debt)'

109 'And I wyll be thy true servaunte, (servant)
And trewely serve the,
Tyl ye have foure hondred pounde
Of money good and free.'

110 The abbot sware a full grete othe,
'By God that dyed on a tree,
Get the londe where thou may,
For thou getest none of me.'

111 'By dere worthy God,' then sayd the knyght,
'That all this world wrought,
But I have my londe agayne, (Unless, land
Full dere it shall be bought.'

112 'God, that was of a mayden borne,
Leve vs well to spede!
For it is good to assay a frende (test)
Or that a man have nede.' (Before)

113 The abbot lothely on hym gan loke,
And vylaynesly hym gan call; (villainously)
'Out,' he sayd, 'Thou fals knyght,
Spede the out of my hall!'

114 'Thou lyest,' then sayd the gentyll knyght,
'Abbot, in thy hal;
False knyght was I never,
By God that made us all.'

115 Up then stode that gentyll knyght,
To the abbot sayd he,
To suffre a knyght to knele so longe,
Thou canst no curteysye. (lack any manners)

116 In ioustes and in tournement
Full ferre than have I be, (far)
And put my selfe as ferre in prees (far in peril)
As ony that ever I se.

117 'What wyll ye gyve more,' sayd the iustice,
'And the knyght shall make a releyse?
And elles dare I safly swere
Ye holde never your londe in pees.' (Peace)

118 'An hondred pounde,' sayd the abbot;
The justice sayd, Gyve hym two;
'Nay, be God,' sayd the knyght,
'Yit gete ye it not so.'

119 'Though ye wolde gyve a thousand more,
Yet were ye never the nere; (near settlement)
Shall there never be myn heyre (heir)
Abbot, iustice, ne frere.'

120 He stert hym to a borde anone, (table)
Tyll a table rounde,
And there he shoke oute of a bagge
Even four hundred pound.

121 'Have here thi golde, sir abbot,' saide the knight,

'Which that thou lentest me;
Had thou ben curtes at my comynge, (courteous)
Rewarded shuldest thou have be.'

122 The abbot sat styll, and ete no more,
For all his ryall fare; (royal)
He cast his hede on his shulder,
And fast began to stare.

123 'Take me my golde agayne,' saide the abbot,
'Sir iustice, that I toke the:'
'Not a peni,' said the iustice,
'Bi God, that dyed on tree.'

124 'Sir abbot, and ye men of lawe,
Now have I holde my daye;
Now shall I have my londe agayne,
For ought that you can saye.'

125 The knyght stert out of the dore,
Awaye was all his care,
And on he put his good clothynge,
The other he lefte there.

126 He wente hym forth full mery syngynge, (singing)
As men have tolde in tale;
His lady met hym at the gate,
At home in Verysdale.

127 'Welcome, my lorde,' sayd his lady;
'Syr, lost is all your good?' (everything)
'Be mery, dame,' sayd the knyght,
'And pray for Robyn Hode,'

128 'That ever his soul be in blysse:
He holpe me out of tene; (trouble)

Ne had be his kynd nesse,
Beggers had we bene.'

129 'The abbot and I accorded ben, (agreed)
He is served of his pay;
The god yoman lent it me,
As I cam by the way.'

130 This knight than dwelled fayre at home,
The sothe for to saye,
Tyll he had gete four hundred pound,
Al redy for to pay.

131 He purveyed him an hundred bowes, (provided)
The stryng s well ydyght, (tight)
An hundred shefe of arow s gode,
The hedys burneshed full bryght;

132 And every arowe an ell longe,
With pecok wel idyght, (fitted)
Inocked all with whyte silver;
It was a semely syght.

133 He purveyed hym an hondreth men,
Well harnessed in that stede,
And hym selfe in that same sete,
And clothed in whyte and rede.

134 He bare a launsgay in his honde, (lance)
And a man ledde his male, (pack)
And reden with a lyght songe
Unto Bernysdale.

135 But as he went at a brydge ther was a wrastelyng, (wrestling)
And there taryed was he, (delayed)
And there was all the best yemen

Of all the west countree.

136 A full fayre game there was up set,
A whyte bulle up i-pyght, (placed)
A grete courser, with sadle and brydil,
With golde burnyssht full bryght.

137 A payre of gloves, a rede golde rynge,
A pype of wyne, in fay; (fact)
What man that bereth hym best i-wys
The prize shall bere away.

138 There was a yoman in that place,
And best worthy was he,
And for he was ferre and frembde bested,
Slayne he shulde have be.

139 The knight had ruthe of this yoman, (pity)
In plac where he stode;
He sayde that yoman shulde have no harme,
For love of Robyn Hode.

140 The knyght presed in to the place,
An hundreth folowed hym frere,
With bowes bent and arowes sharpe,
For to shende that companye. (Destroy)

141 They shulderd all and made hym rome, (room)
To wete what he wolde say; (hear)
He toke the yeman bi the hande,
And gave hym al the play.

142 He gave hym fyve marke for his wyne, (marks)
There it lay on the molde, (ground)
And bad it shulde be set a broche, (tapped)
Drynk who so wolde.

143 Thus longe taried this gentyll knyght,
Tyll that play was done;
So longe abode Robyn fastinge,
Thre houres after the none.

The Third Fytte

144 Lyth and lystyn, gentilmen,
All that nowe be here;
Of Litell Johnn, that was the knight s man, (servant)
Goode myrth ye shall here. (Hear)
145 It was upon a mery day
That yonge men wolde go shete; (shooting)
Lytell Johnn fet his bowe anone, (anon)
And sayde he wolde them mete.

146 Thre tymes Litell Johnn shet aboute,
And alway he slet the wande; (split the stick)
The proud sherif of Notingham
By the mark s can stande.

147 The sherif swore a full greate othe:
'By hym that dyede on a tre,
This man is the best arschere (archer)
That ever yet sawe I me.'

148 'Say me nowe, wight yonge man, (brave)
What is nowe thy name?
In what countre were thou borne,
And where is thy wonynge wane?' (dwelling)

149 'In Holdernes, sir, I was borne,
I-wys al of my dame;
Men cal me Reynolde Gren lef
Whan I am at hame.'

150 'Sey me, Reynolde Gren lefe,
Wolde thou dwell with me?
And every yere I woll the gyve
Twenty marke to thy fee.'

151 'I have a maister,' sayde Litell Johnn,
'A curteys knight is he;
May ye leve gete of hym,
The better may it be.'

152 The sherif gate Litell John
Twelve monethes of the knight; (months)
Therfore he gave him right anone (anon)
A gode hors and a wight. (Strong)

153 Nowe is Litell John the sherif s man,
God lende us well to spede! (Help us)
But alwey thought Lytell John
To quyte hym wele his mede.(grant, his due)

154 'Nowe so God me help' sayde Litell John,
'And by my true leutye,
I shall be the worst servaunt to hym
That ever yet had he.'

155 fell upon a Wednesday
The sherif on huntynge was gone,
And Litel Iohn lay in his bed,
And was foriete at home. (Forgotten)

156 Therfore he was fastinge
Til it was past the none;
'Gode sir stuarde, I pray to the, (steward)
Gyve me my dynere,' saide Litell John.

157 'It is longe for Grenelefe
Fastinge thus for to be;
Therfor I pray the, sir stuarde,
Mi dyner gif me.'

158 'Shalt thou never ete ne drynke,' saide the stuarde,
'Tyll my lorde be come to towne:'
'I make myn avowe to God,' saide Litell John,
'I had lever to crake thy crowne.' (would rather)

159 The boteler was full uncurteys, (butler)
There he stode on flore;
He start to the botery
And shet fast the dore.

160 Lytell Johnn gave the boteler suche a tap
His backe went nere in two;
Though he lived an hundred ier, (years)
The wors shuld he go.

161 He sporned the dore with his fote;
It went open wel and fyne;
And there he made large lyveray, (took, helping)
Bothe of ale and of wyne.

162 'Sith ye wol nat dyne,' sayde Litell John, (after)
'I shall gyve you to drinke;
And though ye lyve an hundred wynter,
On Lytel Johnn ye shall thinke.'

163 Litell John ete, and Litel John drank,
The whil that he wolde;
The sherife had in his kechyn a coke, (cook)
A stoute man and a bolde.

164 'I make myn avowe to God,' saide the coke,
'Thou arte a shrewde hynde
In ani hous for to dwel,
For to ask thus to dyne.'

165 And there he lent Litell John (gave)
God strokis thre; (blows)
'I make myn avowe to God,' sayde Lytell John,
'These strokis lyked well me.'

166 'Thou arte a bolde man and hardy,
And so thinketh me;
And or I pas fro this place (before)
Assayed better shalt thou be.' (Tested)

167 Lytell Johnn drew a ful gode sworde,
The coke toke another in hande;
They thought no thynge for to fle,
But stifly for to stande.

168 There they faught sore togedere
Two myl way and well more; (two miles)
Myght neyther other harme done,
The mountnaunce of an owre. (for an hour)

169 'I make myn avowe to God,' sayde Litell Johnn,
And by my true lewté
Thou art one of the best sworde-men
That ever yit sawe I me.

170 'Cowdest thou shote as well in a bowe,
To grene wode thou shuldest with me, (greenwood)
And two times in the yere thy clothinge
Chaunged shuld be;'

171 'And every yere of Robyn Hode

Twenty merke to thy fe:' (fee, pay)
'Put up thy swerde,' saide the coke,
'And felow s woll we be.'

172 Thanne he fet to Lytell Johnn (brought)
The nowmbles of a do, (sweetbreads)
Gode brede, and full gode wyne;
They ete and drank theretoo.

173 And when they had dronkyn well,
Theyre trouth s togeder they plight
That they wolde be with Robyn
That ylk sam nyght. (Very)

174 They dyd them to the tresoure-hows,
As fast as they myght gone;
The lokk s, that were of full gode stele, (good steel)
They brake them everichone. (every one)

175 They toke away the silver vessell,
And all that they might get;
Pecis, masars, ne sponis, (dishes, cups, spoons)
Wolde thei not forget.

176 Also they toke the god pens, (pence, coins
Thre hundred pounde and more,
And did them streyte to Robyn Hode, (went)
Under the grene wode hore. (Ancient)

177 'God the save, my der mayster,
And Criste the saue and se!' (watch over)
And thanne sayde Robyn to Litell Johnn,
Welcome myght thou be.

178 'Also be that fayre yeman
Thou bryngest there with the;

What tydyngs fro Notyngham?
Lytill Johnn, tell thou me.'

179 'Well the gretith the proud sheryf, (greets you)
And sendeth the here by me
His coke and his silver vessell, (cook)
And thre hundred pounde and thre.'

180 'I make myne avowe to God,' sayde Robyn,
'And to the Trenyté, (Trinity)
It was never by his gode wyll (sheriff's good will)
This gode is come to me.'

181 Lytyll Johnn there hym bethought
On a shrewde wyle; (plan)
Fyve myle in the forest he ran,
Hym happed all his wyll. (his plan came off)

182 Than he met the proud sheref,
Huntynge with houndes and horne;
Lytell Johnn coude of curtesye, (knew)
And knelyd hym beforne.

183 'God the save, my der mayster,
And Criste the save and se!' (watch over)
'Reynolde Gren lefe,' sayde the shryef,
'Where hast thou nowe be?'

184 'I have be in this forest;
A fayre syght can I se;
It was one of the fayrest syghtes
That ever yet sawe I me.'

185 'Yonder I sawe a ryght fayre harte, (male red deer)
His coloure is of grene;

Seven score of dere upon a herde
Be with hym all bydene. (Together)'

186 'Their tynds are so sharpe, maister, (horns)
Of sexty, and well mo,
That I durst not shote for drede,
Lest they wolde me slo.' (Slay)

187 'I make myn avowe to God,' sayde the shyref,
'That syght wolde I fayne se:'
'Buske you thyderwarde, mi der mayster, (hurry)
Anone, and wende with me.'

188 The sherif rode, and Litell Johnn
Of fote he was smerte, (quick)
And whane they came before Robyn,
'Lo, sir, here is the mayster-herte.'

189 Still stode the proud sherief,
A sory man was he;
'Wo the worthe, Raynolde Gren lefe,
Thou hast betrayed nowe me.'

190 'I make myn avowe to God,' sayde Litell Johnn,
'Mayster, ye be to blame;
I was mysserved of my dynere (deprived)
Whan I was with you at home.'

191 Sone he was to souper sette,
And served well with silver white,
And whan the sherif sawe his vessell,
For sorowe he myght nat ete.

192 'Make glad chere,' sayde Robyn Hode,
'Sherif, for charité,

And for the love of Litill Johnn
Thy lyfe I graunt to the.'

193 Whan they had souped well,
The day was al gone;
Robyn commaunded Litell Johnn
To drawe of his hosen and his shone; (hose and shoes)

194 His kirtell, and his cote of pie, (tunic, multicoloured)
That was fured well and fine,
And toke hym a grene mantel, (gave)
To lap his body therin. (wrap)

195 Robyn commaundyd his wight yonge men,
under the grene-wode tree,
They shulde lye in that same sute, (wear)
That the sherif myght them see.

196 All nyght lay the proud sherif
In his breche and in his schert; (breeches, shirt)
No wonder it was, in grene wode,
Though his syds gan to smerte. (Ache)

197 'Make glade chere,' sayde Robyn Hode,
'Sheref, for charité
For this is our ordre iwys,
Under the grene wode tree.'

198 'This is harder order,' sayde the sherief,
'Than any ankir or frere; (hermit or monk)
For all the golde in mery Englonde
I wolde nat longe dwell her.'

199 'All this twelue monthes,' sayde Robin,
'Thou shalt dwell with me;

I shall the teche, proud sherif,
An outlaw for to be.'

200 'Or I be here another nyght,' sayde the sherif, (before)
'Robyn, nowe pray I the,
Smyte of mijn hede rather to-morowe, (strike off my head)'
And I forgyve it the.

201 'Lat me go,' than sayde the sherif,
'For saynt charité
And I woll be the best frende
That ever yet had ye.'

202 'Thou shalt swere me an othe,' sayde Robyn,
'On my bright bronde; (sword)
Shalt thou never awayte me scathe, (plot to harm me)
By water ne by lande.'

203 'And if thou fynde any of my men,
By nyght or by day,
Upon thyn oth thou shalt swere
To helpe them that thou may.' (as far as)

204 Nowe hathe the sherif sworne his othe,
And home he began to gone;
He was as full of grene wode
As ever was hepe of stone. (Fruit)

The Fourth Fytte

205 The sherif dwelled in Notingham;
He was fayne he was agone; (glad)
And Robyn and his mery men
Went to wode anone.

206 'Go we to dyner,' sayde Littell Johnn;
Robyn Hode sayde, Nay;
For I drede Our Lady be wroth with me,
Foe she sent me nat my pay.

207 'Have no doute, maister,' sayde Litell Johnn;
'Yet is nat the sonne at rest;
For I dare say, and savely swere, (safely)
The knight is true and truste.'

208 'Take thy bowe in thy hande,' sayde Robyn,
'Late Much wende with the, (go)
And so shal Wyllyam Scarlok,
And no man abyde with me.'

209 'And walke up under the Sayles,
And to Watlynge-strete,
And wayte after some unketh gest; (stranger)
Up-chaunce ye may them mete.'
210 'Whether he be messengere,
Or a man that myrthes can, (entertain)
Of my good he shall have some,
Yf he be a por man.'

211 Forth then stert Lytel Johan,
Half in tray and tene, (anger and indignation)
And gyrde hym with a full good swerde,
Under a mantel of grene.

212 They went up to the Sayles,
These yemen all thre;
They loked est, they loked west,
They myght no man se.

213 But as they loked in Bernysdale,
By the hye waye,

Than were they ware of two blacke monkes,
Eche on a good palferay.

214 Then bespake Lytell Johan,
To Much he gan say,
I dare lay my lyfe to wedde, (as a pledge)
That these monkes have brought our pay.

215 'Make glad chere,' sayd Lytell Johan,
'And drese your bowes of ewe, (prepare)
And loke your hert s be seker and sad, (sure and steadfast)
Your stryngs trusty and trewe.'

216 'The monke hath two and fifty men,
And seven somers full stronge; (pack horses)
There rydeth no bysshop in this londe
So ryally, I understond.'

217 'Brethern,' sayd Lytell Johan,
'Here are no more but we thre;
But we bryng them to dyner, (unless)
Our mayster dare we not se.'

218 'Bende your bowes,' sayd Lytell Johan,
'Make all yon prese to stonde; (crowd)
The formost monke, his lyfe and his deth
Is closed in my honde. (Held)'

219 'Abyde, chorle monke,' sayd Lytell Johan, (crude)
'No ferther that thou gone; (go)
Yf thou doost, by dere worthy God,
Thy deth is in my honde.'

220 'And evyll luck on thy hede,' sayd Lytell Johan,
'Ryght under thy hattes bonde; (hat band)

For thou hast made our mayster wroth,
He is fastynge so longe.'

221 'Who is your mayster?' sayd the monke;
Lytell Johan sayd, Robyn Hode;
'He is a stronge thefe,' sayd the monke,
'Of hym herd I never good.'

222 'Thou lyest,' than sayd Lytell Johan,
'And that shall rew the; (you will regret)
He is a yeman of the forest,
To dyne he hath bode the.' (Bidden)

223 Much was redy with a bolte, (arrow)
Redly and anone,
He set the monke to-fore the brest,
To the grounde that he can gone. (he dismounted)

224 Of two and fyfty wyght yonge yemen (brave)
There abode not one,
Saf a lytell page and a grome, (except, groom)
To lede the somers with Lytel Johan.

225 They brought the monke to the lodge dore,
Whether he were loth or lefe, (wanted to or not)
For to speke with Robyn Hode,
Maugré in theyr tethe. (Notwithstanding)

226 Robyn dyde adowne his hode, (lowered)
The monke whan that he se;
The monke was not so curteyse,
His hode then let he be.

227 'He is a chorle, mayster, by dere worthy God,.'(churl)
Than sayd Lytell Johan:

'Thereof no force,' sayd Robyn, (no matter)
'For curteysy can he none.'

228 'How many men,' sayd Robyn,
'Had this monke, Johan?'
'Fyfty and two whan that we met,
But many of them be gone.'

229 'Let blowe a horne,' sayd Robyn,
'That felaushyp may us knowe;'
Seven score of wyght yemen (brave)
Came pryckynge on a rowe. (hurrying)

230 And everych of them a good mantell
Of scarlet and of raye; (striped)
All they came to good Robyn,
To wyte what he wolde say. (Learn)

231 They made the monke to wasshe and wype,
And syt at his denere,
Robyn Hode and Lytell Johan
They served him both infere. (as an equal)

232 'Do gladly, monke,' sayd Robyn.
'Gramercy, syr,' sayd he. (thank you)
'Where is your abbay, whan ye are at home,
And who is your avow?'

233 'Saynt Mary abbay,' sayd the monke,
'Though I be symple here.'
'In what offyce?' sayd Robyn:
'Syr, the hye selerer.' (Cellarer)

234 'Ye be the more welcome,' sayd Robyn,
'So ever mote I the; (met)
Fyll of the best wyne,' sayd Robyn,

'This monke shall drynke to me.'

235 'But I have grete mervayle,' sayd Robyn,
'Of all this long day;
I drede Our Lady be wroth with me,
She sent me not my pay.'

236 'Have no doute, mayster,' sayd Lytell Johan,
'Ye have no nede, I saye;
This monke it hath brought, I dare well swere,
For he is of her abbay.'

237 'And she was a borowe,' sayd Robyn, (security)
'Betwene a knyght and me,
Of a lytell money that I hym lent,
Under the grene wode tree.'

238 'And yf thou hast that sylver i-brought,
I pray the let me se;
And I shall help the eftsones, (in return)
Yf thou have nede to me.'

239 The monke swore a full grete othe,
With a sory chere, (face)
'Of the borowehode thou spekest to me, (security)
Herde I never ere.'

240 'I make myn avowe to God,' sayd Robyn,
'Monke, thou art to blame;
For God is holde a ryghtwys man,
And so is his dame.'

241 'Thou toldest with thyn own tonge,
Thou may not say nay,
How thou arte her servaunt,
And servest her every day.'

242 'And thou art made her messengere,
My money for to pay;
Therfore I cun the mor thanke
Thou arte come at thy day.'

243 'What is in your cofers?' sayd Robyn,
'Trewe than tell thou me:'
'Syr,' he sayd, 'Twenty marke,
Al so mote I the.'

244 'Yf there be no more,' sayd Robyn,
'I wyll not one peny;
Yf thou hast myster of ony more, (need)
Syr, more I shall lende to the.'

245 'And yf I fynd more,' sayd Robyn,
'Iwys thou shalte it for gone;
For of thy spendynge sylver, monke, (silver, money)
Thereof wyll I ryght none.'

246 'Go nowe forthe, Lytell Johan,
And the trouth tell thou me;
If there be no more but twenty marke,
No peny that I se.'

247 Lytell Johan spred his mantell downe,
As he had done before,
And he tolde out of the monkes male (valise)
Eyght hondred pounde and more.

248 Lytell Johan let it lye full styll,
And went to his mayster in hast;
'Syr,' he sayd, 'The monke is trewe ynowe,
Our Lady hath doubled your cast.' (Loan)

249 'I make myn avowe to God,' sayd Robyn
'Monke, what tolde I the?'
Our Lady is the trewest woman
That ever yet founde I me.

250 'By dere worthy God,' sayd Robyn,
'To seche all Englond thorowe,
Yet founde I never to my pay
A moche better borowe.'

251 'Fyll of the best wyne, and do hym drynke,' sayd Robyn,
'And grete well thy lady hende, (gracious)
And yf she have nede to Robyn Hode,
A frende she shall hym fynde.'

252 'And yf she nedeth ony more sylver,
Come thou agayne to me,
And, by this token she hath me sent,
She shall have such thre.'

253 The monke was goynge to London ward,
There to holde grete mote, (meeting)
The knyght that rode so hye on hors,
To brynge hym under fote.

254 'Whether be ye away?' sayd Robyn:
'Syr, to maners in this londe, (manors)
Too reken with our reves,
That have done moch wronge.'

255 'Come now forth, Lytell Johan,
And harken to my tale;
A better yemen I knowe none,
To seke a monk s male.' (Valise)

256 'How moch is in yonder other corser?' sayd Robyn,
'The soth must we see:' (truth)
'By Our Lady,' than sayd the monke,
'That were no curteysye,'

257 'To bydde a man to dyner, (invite)
And syth hym bete and bynde.' (later)
'It is our old maner,' sayd Robyn,
'To leve but lytell behynde.'

258 The monke toke the hors with spore, (spurred on his horse)
No lenger wolde he abyde:
'Ask to drynk' than sayd Robyn, (ask permission)
'Or that ye forther ryde.' (Before)

259 'Nay, for God,' than sayd the monke,
'Me reweth I cam so nere; (rue)
For better chepe I myght have dyned (more cheaply)
In Blythe or in Dankestere.'

260 'Grete well your abbot,' sayd Robyn,
'And your pryour, I you pray,
And byd hym send me such a monke
To dyner every day.'

261 Now lete we that monke be styll,
And speke we of that knyght:
Yet he came to holde his day,
Whyle that it was lyght.

262 He dyde him streyt to Bernysdale, (took himself)
Under the grene wode tre,
And he founde there Robyn Hode,
And all his mery meyné.

263 The knyght lyght doune of his good palfray; (dismounted)
Robyn whan he gan see,
So curteysly he dyde adoune his hode,
And set hym on his knee.

264 'God the save, Robyn Hode,
And all this company:'
'Welcome be thou, gentyll knyght,
And ryght welcome to me.'

265 Than bespake hym Robyn Hode,
To that knyght so fre:
What ned dryveth the to grene wode?
I praye the, syr knyght, tell me.

266 'And welcome be thou, gentyll knyght,
Why hast thou be so longe?'
'For the abbot and the hye iustyce
Wolde have had my londe.'

267 'Hast thou thy londe agayne?' sayd Robyn;
'Treuth than tell thou me:'
'Ye, for God,' sayd the knyght,
'And that thanke I God and the.'

268 'But take not a grefe that I have be so longe; (be annoyed)
I came by a wrastelynge,
And there I holpe a por yeman, (helped)
With wronge was put behynde.' (Cheated)

269 'Nay, for God,' sayd Robyn,
'Syr knyght, that thanke I the;
What man that helpeth a good yeman,
His frende than wyll I be.'

270 'Have here foure hondred pounde,'
'The whiche ye lent to me;
And here is also twenty marke
For your curteysy.'

271 'Nay, for God,' than sayd Robyn,
'Thou broke it well for ay; (enjoy it well for ever)
For Our Lady, by her hye selerer, (high cellarer)
Hath sent to me my pay.'

272 'And yf I toke it i-twyse, (twice)
A shame it were to me;
But trewely, gentyll knyght,
Welcom arte thou to me.'

273 Whan Robyn had tolde his tale,
He leugh and had good chere: (laughed)
'By my trouthe,' then sayd the knyght,
'Your money is redy here.'

274 'Broke it well,' sayd Robyn, (enjoy)
'Thou gentyll knyght so fre;
And welcome be thou, gentyll knyght,
Under my trystell-tre. (meeting tree)'

275 'But what shall these bowes do?' sayd Robyn,
'And these arowes ifedred fre?' (feathered)
'By God,' than sayd the knyght,
'A por present to the.'

276 'Come now forth, Lytell Johan,
And go to my tresuré,
And brynge me there foure hondred pounde;
The monke over-tolde it me. (over-paid)'

277 'Have here foure hondred pounde,
Thou gentyll knyght and trewe,
And bye hors and harnes good, (horse and harness)
And gylte thy spores all newe. (Gild)'

278 'And yf thou fayle ony spendynge, (lack)
Com to Robyn Hode,
And by my trouth thou shalt none fayle,
The whyles I have any good. (While)'

279 'And broke well thy foure hondred pound, (enjoy)
Whiche I lent to the,
And make thy selfe no more so bare,
By the counsell of me.'

280 Thus than holpe hym good Robyn, (helped)
The knyght all of his care:
God, that syt in heven hye,
Graunte us well to fare!

The Fifth Fytte

281 Now hath the knyght his leve i-take,
And wente hym on his way;
Robyn Hode and his mery men
Dwelled styll full many a day. (Quietly)
282 Lyth and lysten, gentil men,
And herken what I shall say,
How the proud sheryfe of Notyngham
Dyde crye a full fayre play;

283 That all the best archers of the north
Sholde come upon a day,
And he that shoteth allther best (best of all)
The game shall bere a way.

284 He that shoteth allther best,
Furthest fayre and lowe,
At a payre of fynly buttes, (fine)
Under the grene wode shawe, (thicket)

285 A ryght good arowe he shall have,
The shaft of sylver whyte,
The hede and the feders of ryche red golde, (feathers)
In Englond is none lyke.

286 This than herde good Robyn,
Under his trystell-tre:
'Make you redy, ye wyght yonge men; (brave)
That shotynge wyll I se.'
287 'Buske you, my mery yonge men, (Hurry)
Ye shall go with me;
And I wyll wete the sheryfes fayth, (test)
Trewe and yf he be.'

288 Whan they had theyr bowes i-bent,
Theyr takles fedred fre, (feathered arrows)
Seven score of wyght yonge men
Stode by Robyns knc.

289 Whan they cam to Notyngham,
The buttes were fayre and longe;
Many was the bolde archere
That shoted with bow s stronge.

290 'There shall but syx shote with me;
The other shal kepe my heuede, (protect my head)
And stand with good bow s bent,
That I be not desceyved.' (Deceived)

291 The fourth outlawe his bowe gan bende,
And that was Robyn Hode,

And that behelde the proud sheryfe,
All by the but as he stode.

292 Thryes Robyn shot about,
And alway he slist the wand,
And so dyde good Gylberte
Wyth the whyt hande.

293 Lytell Johan and good Scatheloke
Were archers good and fre;
Lytell Much and good Reynolde,
The worste wolde they not be. (Would)

294 Whan they had shot aboute,
These archours fayre and good,
Evermore was the best,
For soth, Robyn Hode.

295 Hym was delyvered the good arowe, (awarded)
For best worthy was he;
He toke the yeft so curteysly, (prize)
To grene wode wolde he.

296 They cryed out on Robyn Hode,
And grete hornes gan they blowe:
'Wo worth the, treason!' sayd Robyn,
'Full evyl thou art to knowe. (Evil)'

297 'And wo be thou! thou proud sheryf,
Thus gladdynge thy gest; (pleasing)
Other wyse thou behot me (promised)
In yonder wylde forest.'

298 'But had I the in grene wode,
Under my trystell-tre,

Thou sholdest leve me a better wedde (pledge)
Than thy trewe lewté.'

299 Full many a bow there was bent,
And arow s let they glyde;
Many a kyrtell there was rent, (tunic)
And hurt many a syde.

300 The outlawes shot was so stronge
That no man myght them dryve,
And the proud sheryf s men,
They fled away full blyue. (Quickly)

301 Robyn sawe the busshement to-broke, (ambush)
In grene wode he wolde have be;
Many an arowe there was shot
Amonge that company.

302 Lytell Johan was hurte full sore,
With an arowe in his kne,
That he myght neyther go nor ryde;
It was full grete pyté.

303 'Mayster,' then sayd Lytell Johan,
'If ever thou lovest me,
And for that ylke lord's love (same)
That dyed upon a tre,'

304 'And for the medes of my servyce, (rewards)
That I have served the,
Lete never the proud sheryf
Alyve now fynde me.'

305 'But take out thy brown swerde, (blood stained)
And smyte all of my hede,
And gyve me woundes depe and wyde;

No lyfe on me be lefte.'

306 'I wolde not that,' sayd Robyn,
'Johan, that thou were slawe,
For all the golde in mery Englonde,
Though it lay now on a rawe.' (in a row)

307 'God forbede,' sayd Lytell Much,
'That dyed on a tre,
That thou sholdest, Lytell Johan,
Parte our company.' (Depart)

308 Up he toke hym on his backe,
And bare hym well a myle;
Many a tyme he layd hym downe,
And shot another whyle.

309 Then was there a fayre castell, (castle)
A lytell within the wode;
Double-dyched it was about,
And walled, by the rode. (Cross)

310 And there dwelled that gentyll knyght,
Syr Rychard at the Lee,
That Robyn had lent his good, (money)
Under the grene-wode tree.

311 In he toke good Robyn,
And all his company:
'Welcome be thou, Robyn Hode,
Welcome arte thou to me;'

312 'And moche I thanke the of thy confort,
And of thy curteysye,
And of thy grete kyndenesse,
Under the grene wode tre.'

313 'I love no man in all this worlde
So much as I do the;
For all the proud sheryf of Notyngham, (Despite)
Ryght here shalt thou be.'

314 'Shyt the gates, and drawe the brydge,
And let no man come in,
And arme you well, and make you redy,
And to the walles ye wynne. (make your way)'

315 'For one thynge, Robyn, I the behote; (promise)
I swere by Saynt Quyntyne, (Quentin)
These forty dayes thou wonnest with me, (dwell)
To soupe, ete, and dyne.'

316 Bordes were layde, and clothes were spredde,
Redely and anone;
Robyn Hode and his mery men
To mete can they gone

The Sixth Fytte

317 Lythe and lysten, gentylmen,
And herkyn to your songe;
Howe the proud shyref of Notyngham,
And men of armys stronge,

318 Full fast cam to the hye shyref,
The contré up to route, (rouse)
And they besette the knyghtes castell, (besieged)
The walles all aboute.

319 The proud shyref loude gan crye,
And sayde, Thou traytour knight,
Thou kepest here the kynges enemys,
Agaynst the lawe and right.

320 'Syr, I wyll avowe that I have done, (admit)
The dedys that here be dyght, (done)
Upon all the landes that I have,
As I am a trew knyght.'

321 'Wende furth, sirs, on your way, (Go forth)
And do no more to me
Tyll ye wyt oure kynges wille, (know)
What he wyll say to the.'
322 The shyref thus had his answere,
Without any lesynge; (lying)
Furth he yede to London towne, (went)
All for to tel our kinge.

323 Ther he telde him of that knight,
And eke of Robyn Hode,
And also of the bolde archars,
That were soo noble and gode.

324 'He wyll avowe that he hath done, (admit)
To mayntene the outlawes stronge;
He wyll be lorde, and set you at nought,
In all the northe londe.'

325 'I wil be at Notyngham,' saide our kynge,
'Within this fourteenyght,
And take I wyll Robyn Hode,
And so I wyll that knight.'

326 'Go nowe home, shyref,' sayde our kynge,
'And do as I byd the;
And ordeyn gode archers ynowe, (organise, enough)
Of all the wyd contré.' (From)

327 The shyref had his leve i-take,
And went hym on his way,

And Robyn Hode to grene wode,
Vpon a certen day.

328 And Lytel John was hole of the arowe (healed)
That shot was in his kne,
And dyd hym streyght to Robyn Hode,
Under the grene wode tree.

329 Robyn Hode walked in the forest,
Under the levys grene;
The proud shyref of Notyngham
Thereof he had grete tene. (anger)

330 The shyref there fayled of Robyn Hode, (missed)
He myght not have his pray; (prey)
Than he awayted this gentyll knyght,
Bothe by nyght and day.

331 Ever he wayted the gentyll knyght,
Syr Richarde at the Lee,
As he went on haukynge by the ryver-syde,
And let haukes flee.

332 Toke he there this gentyll knight,
With men of armys stronge,
And led hym to Notyngham warde,
Bounde bothe fote and hande.

333 The sheref sware a full grete othe,
Bi hym that dyed on rode, (the cross)
He had lever than an hundred pound (rather)
That he had Robyn Hode.

334 This harde the knyght s wyfe, (heard)
A fayr lady and a free;
She set hir on a gode palfrey,

To grene wode anone rode she.

335 Whanne she cam in the forest,
Under the grene wode tree,
Fonde she there Robyn Hode,
And al his fayre mene. (company)

336 'God the save, gode Robyn,
And all thy company;
For Our dere Ladyes sake,
A bone graunte thou me. (favour)'

337 'Late never my wedded lorde (Let)
Shamefully slayne be;
He is fast bowne to Notingham warde,
For the love of the.'

338 Anone than saide goode Robyn (at once)
To that lady so fre,
What man hath your lorde take?
'The proud shirif,' then sayde she

339 'The shirif hatt hym take' she sayde
'For soth as I the say;
He is nat yet thre myls
Passed on his way.'

340 Up than sterte gode Robyn,
As man that had ben wode: (furious)
'Buske you, my mery men, (Hurry)
For hym that dyed on rode. (the cross)'

341 'And he that this sorowe forsaketh,
By hym that dyed on tre,
Shall he never in grene wode
No lenger dwel with me.'

342 Sone there were gode bowes bent,
Mo than seven score;
Hedge ne dyche spared they none (Hedge nor Ditch)
That was them before.

343 'I make myn avowe to God,' sayde Robyn,
'The sherif wolde I fayne see;
And if I may hym take,
I-quyte shall it be.' (avenged)

344 And whan they came to Notingham,
They walked in the strete;
And with the proud sherif i-wys
Sone can they mete.

345 'Abyde, thou proud sherif,' he sayde,
'Abyde, and speke with me;
Of some tidinges of oure kinge
I wolde fayne here of the.'

346 'This seven yere, by dere worthy God,
Ne yede I this fast on fote; (went)
I make myn avowe to God, thou proud sherif,
It is nat for thy gode.'

347 Robyn bent a full goode bowe,
An arrowe he drowe at wyll;
He hit so the proud sherife
Upon the grounde he lay full still.

348 And or he myght up aryse, (before)
On his fete to stonde,
He smote of the sherifs hede (off)
With his bright bronde.

349 'Lye thou there, thou proud sherife,

Evyll mote thou cheue! (Must, end)
There myght no man to the truste
The whyles thou were a lyve.'

350 His men drewe out theyr bryght swerdes,
That were so sharpe and kene,
And layde on the sheryves men,
And dryved them downe bydene. (forthwith)

351 Robyn stert to that knyght, (leapt)
And cut a two his bonde,
And toke hym in his hand a bowe,
And bad hym by hym stonde.

352 'Leve thy hors the behynde,
And lerne for to renne; (run)
Thou shalt with me to grene wode,
Through myr, mosse, and fenne.'
353 'Thou shalt with me to grene wode,
Without ony leasynge, (lying)
Tyll that I have gete us grace
Of Edwarde, our comly kynge.' (from)

The Seventh Fytte

354 The kynge came to Notynghame,
With knyght s in grete araye, (number)
For to take that gentyll knyght
And Robyn Hode, and yf he may.

355 He asked men of that countré
After Robyn Hode,
And after that gentyll knyght,
That was so bolde and stout.

356 Whan they had tolde hym the case
Our kynge understode ther tale,
And seased in his honed (seized)
The knyghtes londes all.
357 All the compasse of Lancasshyre
He went both ferre and nere,
Tyll he came to Plomton Parke;
He faylyd many of his dere. (missed)

358 There our kynge was wont to se
Herd s many one,
He coud unneth fynde one dere, (hardly)
That bare ony good horne.

359 The kynge was wonder wroth withall,
And swore by the Trynyté,
'I wolde I had Robyn Hode,
With eyen I myght hym se.'

360 'And he that wolde smyte of the knyghtes hede,
And brynge it to me,
He shall have the knyghtes londes,
Syr Rycharde at the Le.'

361 'I gyve it hym with my charter,
And sele it with my honde,
To have and holde for ever more,
In all mery Englonde.'

362 Than bespake a fayre olde knyght,
That was treue in his fay: (faith)
A, my leege lorde the kynge, (liege)
One worde I shall you say.

363 There is no man in this countre
May have the knyghtes londes,

Whyle Robyn Hode may ryde of gone,
And bere a bowe in his hondes,

364 That he ne shall lese his hede,
That is the best ball in his hode:
Give it no man, my lorde the kynge,
That ye wyll any good.

365 Half a yere dwelled our comly kynge
In Notyngham, and well more;
Coude he not here of Robyn Hode,
In what countre that he were.

366 But alway went good Robyn
By halke and eke by hyll, (valley, also)
And alway slewe the kyng s dere,
And welt them at his wyll. (used)

367 Than bespake a proude fostere,
That stode by our kynges kne;
Yf ye wyll se good Robyn,
Ye must do after me. (the same as)

368 Take fyve of the best knyghtes
That be in your lede, (party)
And walke downe by yon abbay,
And gete you monkes wede. (habits)

369 And I wyll be your bedesman, (guide)
And lede you the way,
And or ye come to Notyngham, (before)
Myn hede then dare I lay, (wager)

370 That ye shall mete with good Robyn,
On lyve yf that he be;

Or ye come to Notyngham, (Before)
With eyen ye shall hym se.

371 Full hastly our kynge was dyght, (Quickly, directed)
So were his knyghtes fyve,
Everych of them in monke s wede, (Everyone, attire)
And hasted them thyder blyve.

372 Our kynge was grete above his cole, (cowl)
A brode hat on his crowne,
Ryght as he were abbot-lyke,
They rode up into the towne.

373 Styf botes our kynge had on,
Forsoth as I you say;
He rode syngynge to grene wode, (singing)
The covent was clothed in graye. (convent)

374 His male-hors and his grete somers (pack horses)
Folowed our kynge behynde,
Tyll they came to grene wode,
A myle under the lynde. (trees)

375 There they met with good Robyn,
Stondynge on the waye,
And so dyde many a bolde archere,
For soth as I you say.

376 Robyn toke the kynges hors,
Hastely in that stede, (place)
And sayd, Syr abbot, by your leve,
A whyle ye must abyde.

377 'We be yemen of this foreste,
Under the grene wode tre;
We lyve by our kyng s dere,

Under the grene wode tre;'

378 'And ye have chyrches and rentes both,
And gold full grete plente;
Gyve us some of your spendynge,
For saynt charyté.'

379 Than bespake our cumly kynge,
Anone than sayd he;
I brought no more to grene wode
But forty pounde with me.

380 I have layne at Notyngham (stayed)
This fourtynyght with our kynge,
And spent I have full moche good,
On many a grete lordynge.

381 And I have but forty pounde,
No more than have I me;
But yf I had an hondred pounde,
I vouch it half on the.

382 Robyn toke the forty pounde,
And departed it in two partye;
Halfendell he gave his mery men, (Half)
And bad them mery to be.

383 Full curteysly Robyn gan say;
Syr, have this for your spendyng;
We shall mete another day;
'Gramercy,' than sayd our kynge.

384 'But well the greteth Edwarde, our kynge,
And sent to the his seale,
And byddeth the com to Notyngham,
Both to mete and mele' (eat and drink)

385 He toke out the brod targe, (seal)
And sone he lete hym se;
Robyn coud his courteysy, (kwew)
And set hym on his kne.

386 'I love no man in all the worlde
So well as I do my kynge;
Welcome is my lordes seale;
And, monke, for thy tydynge,'

387 'Syr abbot, for thy tydynges,
To day thou shalt dyne with me,
For the love of my kynge,
Under my trystell-tre.' (meeting tree)

388 Forth he lad our comly kynge,
Full fayre by the honde;
Many a dere there was slayne,
And full fast dyghtande. (prepared)

389 Robyn toke a full grete horne,
And loude he gan blowe;
Seven score of wyght yonge men (brave)
Came redy on a rowe.

390 All they kneled on theyr kne,
Full fayre before Robyn:
The kynge sayd hym selfe untyll,
And swore by Saynt Austyn, (Saint Augustine)

391 'Here is a wonder semely syght;
Me thynketh, by Goddes pyne, (pain)
His men are more at his byddynge
Then my men be at myn.'

392 Full hastly was theyr dyner idyght, (prepared)
And therto gan they gone;
They served our kynge with al theyr myght,
Both Robyn and Lytell Johan.

393 Anone before our kynge was set
The fatte venyson,
The good whyte brede, the good rede wyne,
And therto the fyne ale and browne.

394 'Make good chere,' said Robyn,
'Abbot, for charyté;
And for this ylke tydynge,
Blyssed mote thou be. (may)'

395 'Now shalte thou se what lyfe we lede,
Or thou hens wende; (Before you go away)
Than thou may enfourme our kynge,
Whan ye togyder lende.' (dwell)

396 Up they stert all in hast,
Theyr bow s were smartly bent;
Our kynge was never so sore agast,
He wende to have be shente. (thought, killed)

397 Two yerdes there were up set, (rods)
Thereto gan they gange;
By fyfty pase, our kynge sayd,
The merkes were to longe.

398 On every syde a rose-garlonde, (small target)
They shot under the lyne: (trees)
'Who so fayleth of the rose-garlonde,' sayd Robyn,
'His takyll he shall tyne, (tackle, lose)'

399 'And yelde it to his mayster,
Be it never so fyne;
For no man wyll I spare,
So drynke I ale or wyne:'

400 'And bere a buffet on his hede,
Iwys ryght all bare:'
And all that fell in Robyns lote,
He smote them wonder sare. (sore)

401 Twyse Robyn shot a boute,
And ever he cleved the wande, (split)
And so dyde good Gylberte
With the Whyte Hande.

402 Lytell Johan and good Scathelocke,
For nothynge wolde they spare;
When they fayled of the garlonde,
Robyn smote them full sore.

403 At the last shot that Robyn shot,
For all his frendes fare, (success)
Yet he fayled of the garlonde
Thre fyngers and mare.

404 Than bespake good Gylberte,
And thus he gan say;
'Mayster,' he sayd, 'your takyll is lost,
Stande forth and take your pay.' (punishment)

405 'If it be so,' sayd Robyn,
'That may no better be,
Syr abbot, I delyver the myn arowe,
I pray the, syr, serve thou me.'

406 'It falleth not for myn ordre,' sayd our kynge,
'Robyn, by thy leve,
For to smyte no good yeman,
For doute I sholde hym greve.'

407 'Smyte on boldely,' sayd Robyn,
'I give the large leve:' (full permission)
Anone our kynge, with that worde,
He folde up his sleve,

408 And sych a buffet he gave Robyn,
To grounde he yede full nere:
'I make myn avowe to God,' sayd Robyn,
'Thou arte a stalworthe frere.'

409 'There is pith in thyn arme,' sayd Robyn,
'I trowe thou canst well shete:'
Thus our kynge and Robyn Hode
Togeder gan they mete.

410 Robyn beheld our comly kynge
Wystly in the face, (Intently)
So dyde Syr Rycharde at the Le,
And kneled downe in that place.

411 And so dyde all the wylde outlawes,
Whan they se them knele:
'My lorde the kynge of Englonde,
Now I knowe you well.'

412 'Mercy then, Robyn,' sayd our kynge,
'Vnder your trystyll-tre,
Of thy goodnesse and thy grace,
For my men and me!'

413 'Yes, for God,' sayd Robyn,
'And also God me save,
I ask mersy, my lorde the kynge,
And for my men I crave.'

414 'Yes, for God,' than sayd our kynge,
'And therto sent I me, (I Agree)
With that thou leve the grene wode,
And all thy company;'

415 'And come home, syr, to my courte,
And there dwell with me.'
'I make myn avowe to God,' sayd Robyn,
'And ryght so shall it be.'

416 'I wyll come to your courte,
Your servyse for to se,
And brynge with me of my men
Seven score and thre.'

417 'But me lyke well your servyse
I come agayne full soone,
And shote at the donne dere, (brown)
As I am wonte to done.'

The Eighth Fytte

418 'Haste thou ony grene cloth,' sayd our kynge,
'That thou wylte sell nowe to me?'
'Yes, for God,' sayd Robyn,
'Thyrty yerdes and thre.'

419 'Robyn,' sayd our kynge,
'Now pray I the,
Sell me some of that cloth,
To me and my meyné.' (company)

420 'Yes, for God,' then sayd Robyn,
'Or elles I were a fole;
Another day ye wyll me clothe,
I trowe, ayenst the Yole.' (Christmas)

421 The kynge kest of his col then, (cast off his cowl)
A grene garment he dyde on,
And every knyght also, iwys,
Another hode full sone.

422 Whan they were clothed in Lyncolne grene,
They keste away theyr graye;
'Now we shall to Notyngham,'
All thus our kynge gan say.

423 They bente theyr bowes, and forth they went,
Shotynge all in-fere, (together)
Towarde the towne of Notyngham,
Outlawes as they were. (as if)

424 Our kynge and Robyn rode togyder,
For soth as I you say,
And they shote plucke buffet,
As they went by the way.

425 And many a buffet our kynge wan (received)
Of Robyn Hode that day,
And nothynge spared good Robyn
Our kynge in his pay. (payment of buffets)

426 'So God me help' sayd our kynge,
'Thy game is nought to lere; (learn)
I sholde not get a shote of the,
Though I shote all this yere.'

427 All the people of Notyngham
They stode and behelde;
They sawe nothynge but mantels of grene
That covered all the felde.

428 Than every man to other gan say,
I drede our kynge be slone; (slain)
Come Robyn Hode to the towne, iwys
On lyve he lefte never one.

429 Full hastly they began to fle,
Both yemen and knaves,
And olde wyves that myght evyll goo, (hardly walk)
They hypped on theyr staves. (crutches)

430 The kynge loughe full fast, (laughed)
And commaunded them agayne;
When they se our comly kynge,
I-wys they were full fayne. (pleased)

431 They ete and dranke, and made them glad,
And sange with notes hye;
Than bespake our comly kynge
To Syr Rycharde at the Lee.

432 He gave hym there his londe agayne,
A good man he bad hym be;
Robyn thanked our comly kynge,
And set hym on his kne.

433 Had robyn dwelled in the kynges courte
But twelue monethes and thre, (Only)
That he had spent an hondred pounde,
And all his mennes fe. (earnings)

434 In every place where Robyn came

Ever more he layde downe, (paid out)
Both for knyghtes and for squyres,
To gete hym grete renowne.

435. By than the yere was all agone
He had no man but twayne, (two)
Lytell Johan and good Scathlocke,
With hym all for to gone.

436. Robyn sawe yonge men shote
Full ferre upon a day; (far)
'Alas!' than sayd good Robyn,
'My welthe is went away.'

437. 'Somtyme I was an archere good,
A styffe and eke a stronge;
I was compted the best archere (counted)
That was in mery Englonde.'

438. 'Alas!' then sayd good Robyn,
'Alas and well a woo!
Yf I dwele lenger with the kynge,
Sorowe wyll me sloo.' (slay)

439. Forth than went Robyn Hode
Tyll he came to our kynge:
'My lorde the kynge of Englonde,
Graunte me myn askynge.'

440. 'I made a chapell in Bernysdale,
That semely is to se,
It is of Mary Magdaleyne,
And thereto wolde I be.'

441. 'I myght never in this seven nyght
No tyme to slepe ne wynke,

Nother all these seven days (Neither)
Nother ete ne drynke.'

442. 'Me longeth sore to Bernysdale,
I may not be therfro;
Barefote and wolwarde I have hyght (vowed)
Thyder for to go.'

443. 'Yf it be so,' than sayd our kynge,
'It may no better be,
Seven nyght I gyve the leve,
No lengre, to dwell fro me.'

444. 'Gramercy, lorde,' then sayd Robyn,
And set hym on his kne;
He toke his leve full courteysly.
To grene wode then went he.

445. Whan he came to grene wode,
In a mery mornynge,
There he herde the notes small
Of byrdes mery syngynge.

446. 'It is ferre gone,' sayd Robyn, (long time)
'That I was last here;
Me lyste a lytell for to shote (pleases)
At the donne dere.' (brown)

447. Robyn slewe a full grete harte;
His horne than gan he blow,
That all the outlawes of that forest
That horne coud they knowe,

448. And gadred them togyder,
In a lytell throwe. (while)
Seven score of wyght yonge men (brave)

Came redy on a rowe,

1449. And fayre dyde of theyr hodes,
And set them on theyr kne:
'Welcome,' they sayd, 'our mayster,
Under this grene wode tre.'

450. Robyn dwelled in grene wode
Twenty yere and two;
For all drede of Edwarde our kynge,
Agayne wolde he not goo.

451. Yet he was begyled, iwys,
Through a wycked woman,
The pryoresse of Kyrkely,
That nye was of hys kynne:

452. For the love of a knyght,
Syr Roger of Donkesly,
That was her own speciall;
Full evyll mot they the!

453. They toke togyder theyr counsell
Robyn Hode for to sle, (slay)
And how they myght best do that dede,
His banis for to be.

454. Than bespake good Robyn,
In place where as he stode,
'To morow I muste to Kyrkely,
Craftely to be leten blode.' (Skillfully)

455. Syr Roger of Donkestere,
By the pryoresse he lay,
And there they betrayed good Robyn Hode,
Through theyr fals playe.

456. Cryst have mercy on his soule,
That dyed on the rode! (Cross)
For he was a good outlawe,
And dyde pore men moch god.

Illustrations
List of Maps

1. The Gough Map
2. Part of Great North Road on the Gough Map.
3. Jeffery's 1771 map of Yorkshire.
4. Ogilby's Map of part of Great North Road.
5. Barnsdale
6. Robin Hood's route north
7. Sherwood Forest
8. Royal journeys in Lancashire
9. OS Map of Conisbrough
10. Section of Went and Skell valleys.

Details of Maps

Map 1   The Gough Map is drawn on parchment made from two goat skins and is in the custody of the Bodleian Library in Oxford. It is believed have been created over a short period around 1360AD and demonstrates the extent of the general knowledge of England and the limit of English knowledge of Scotland. As with all maps of this period it is drawn with east at the top of the sheet as that is the direction towards Jerusalem.

Map 2   This map shows the alternative routes from York to London superimposed on an extract from the Gough Map. The most direct route does not pass through Sherwood Forest but all routes pass through Barnsdale.

Map 3   This map is a copy of part of the map of Yorkshire produced by Thomas Jeffery in 1771 and covering part of central Barnsdale. It should be noted that the River Went is clearly named whereas the Skell is not.

Map 4   John Ogilby's maps were published towards the end of the seventeenth century This particular map shows a 32-mile-long section of the Great North Road from a point three miles south of Grantham to Tuxford. The map is drawn in three sections, the southern-most point is at the bottom of the left-hand section is at the top of the righthand section. It is clear from this map that the main road from London to the north did not pass through Sherwood Forest.

Map 5   This map of Barnsdale shows details of the local topography and the alignment of Ermine Street and the two routes both called Watling Street.

Map 6   The line on this map marked as a track is the straight line from Nottingham to Wentbridge through Sherwood Forest which would probably have been followed by Robin Hood when fleeing from the Sheriff of Nottingham after the archery contest. It passes within half a mile of Conisbrough Castle.

Map 7   A general map of Sherwood Forest which shows very few main routes running north to south through the forest.

Map 8   Map shows the routes taken in Lancashire by the three King Edwards during the fourteenth and fifteenth centuries. None of them passed through Wyresdale or close to the hamlet of Lee.

Map 9   This map is an enlarged extract from Ordnance Survey Sheet Explorer 279 'Doncaster' showing part of the town of Conisbrough. This map clearly shows the double defensive ditches surrounding the castle and the close proximity of the Anglo-Saxon preaching cross (rood) in the parish churchyard.

Map 10   Although listed as a map this illustration in fact shows two sections, both drawn at the same exaggerated vertical scale and taken through Barnsdale showing the difference between the valleys of the River Went and the Skell. The Went valley is clearly the most notable feature.

List of Photographs

1	View over Barnsdale
2-3	Typical lowland heath.
4-8	Brockadale
9-11	Wentbridge Viaduct
12-15	Went Valley.
16	View over Wentbridge from Sayles
17	Multiple track north side of Went valley.
18-19	Wentbridge village
20	Great North Road, north of Wentbridge.
21-23	The Skell and Skelldale
24	Sleep Hill
25	Watling Street.
26-27	Gorple Road.
28-31	Campsall Church.
32-35	Conisbrough Castle.
36-37	North Bank of RiverAire.
38	Ruins of St Mary's Abbey, York
39-42	Wensleydale – (Verysdale)

Details of Photographs

Photo 1 View west from author's former office over Barnsdale. Village one mile distant is Badsworth, which probably defines the western boundary of Barnsdale.

Photo 2 This photograph shows typical heathland vegetation. Following intense cultivation over the last few centuries the heathland vegetation which covered most of the area occupied by Sherwood Forest has now been almost completely replaced by agricultural or urban development. This photograph was taken in Cannock Chase, about sixty miles southwest of Sherwood and shows fallow deer grazing on heather shoots.

Photo 3 Silver birch trees on heathland in another former royal forest: 'The New Forest'.

Photo 4 Long Crag a near vertical rocky outcrop forming part of the north side of Brockadale, a site of special scientific interest, and believed to be the location of Robin's beloved 'Greenwood'.

Photo 5 The limestone outcrop forming the top of the very steep north wall of Brockadale.

Photo 6 The top of the steep slope which the Great North Road descended before railway engineering techniques were used in the early nineteenth century to excavate a cutting, thereby reducing the gradient of the road.

Photo 7   These water meadows were probably the only part of Brockadale which could be cultivated. The maximum width here is little more than100 yards.

Photo 8   Hunter's Bridge carries the public footpath over the River Went in Brockadale.

Photo 9   Wentbridge Viaduct, constructed in 1963, bypasses the village of Wentbridge and carries the Great North Road over the Went Valley. The steep thickly wooded valley ides are evident. Before the viaduct was constructed the road had to descend the side of the valley.

Photo 10 Another view of the viaduct highlighting the steep valley sides compared to the flat level valley floor.

Photo 11 The viaduct from above. It can be seen that the valley would be almost invisible from any viewpoint other than a location within the valley itself. A feature which could be beneficial if considered from a possible defensive position.

Photo 12 The view of the Went Valley looking downstream from the viaduct. Here the valley widens as it approaches the village of Wentbridge.

Photo 13 This photograph is a repeat of photo 12 annotated to show the direction of flow and probable course of the river before being diverted by drainage improvement works carried out since the Jeffery's 1771 map was drawn.

Photo 14 Between Wentbridge Village and Brockadale the river valley widens slightly.

Photo 15 In places the valley floor becomes overgrown and subject to flooding. However the valley sides remain very steep.

Photo 16 View from Sayles over Wentbridge. It is clear that it would not be possible to see individual travellers passing through the village on the main road. The view of the road is obstructed not only by the form of the land but also by the buildings making up the village. This confirms that Robin did not tell Little John and his companions to climb Sayles to look for travellers but he told them to go upstream.

Photo 17 This was possibly the route of Watling Street before the cutting was excavated and the road upgraded in the early nineteenth century. This is now a public bridleway but it gives a clear picture of how one of the multiple tracks which no doubt formed the main road here would have appeared. It also demonstrates how the 'dern strete' described in the Gest provided cover for Sir Richard at the Lee as he approached Wentbridge.

Photo 18 The Great North Road passing through Wentbridge village at the present time. It is easy to image the congestion which would have been created before the bypass and the viaduct were constructed in 1963.

Photo 19 The Blue Bell Inn situated on the Great North Road at the southern end of Wentbridge was rebuilt in 1974 its history extends long before that. It is recorded that the inn-keeper's licence was rescinded in the early seventeenth century for 'harbouring footpads and ne'er-do-wells', but was restored in 1633. Clearly Wentbridge was a favourite place for highway robbers to operate.

Photo 20 The main road heading north out of Wentbridge towards York. This is the road as constructed in the early eighteen hundreds when the gradient had been markedly reduced, nevertheless the slope can be estimated by comparing the coursing of the upper stone wall on the left-hand side. The earlier gradient is indicated by the original ground level behind the building on the left.

Photo 21 The Skell flowing through Skellow only 500 yards from the point where it merges with the Hampole Beck to form the Old Eabeck. At this point it is about six to eight feet wide and a few inches deep. It is not the major water course implied by Holt in his descriptions.

Photo 22 The Skell pictured in Skellow just west of the Great North Road. The road here is named on the maps as the Roman Ridge. It is constructed on a shallow embankment presumably to overcome problems caused by difficult, marshy ground conditions.

Photo 23 This photograph shows the very shallow, insignificant valley of the Skell which it is claimed by others, probably incorrectly, as to be the 'dale' included in the make-up of the name Barnsdale.

Photo 24 Sleep Hill, which was the location of Robin Hood's Stone mentioned in a deed dated 1422 and held in the archives of Monk Bretton Priority near Barnsley.

Photo 25 Watling Street north of Barnsdale Bar demonstrating clearly the typical straight alignment of the original Roman road. The road is constructed on a low embankment. It is noted on current Ordnance Survey maps and is also known locally as 'Roman Ridge'.

Photo 26 Gorple Road, a historic, probably medieval direct route across the Pennines between Haworth in Yorkshire and Ightenhill in Lancashire. The difficulties of cross Pennine travel are clearly demonstrated.

Photo 27 Another section of Gorple Road.

Photo 28 The west front of Campsall Parish Church, dedicated to Saint Mary Magdalene and believed to be the 'chapel in Barnsdale' which Robin claimed to have 'made'. The main nave of the church is Norman but the tower is obviously much later.

Photo 29 This view of Campsall Church shows the older Norman part of the church to the left of the red bins and the chancel to the right of the bins. It is not necessary to be a student of architecture to notice the difference between the style and the workmanship of the nave and the chancel which was added in the thirteenth or fourteenth century, probably during Robin's lifetime and possibly with his assistance, both physical and financial.

Photo 30 A view of the connection between the nave and the chancel but on the north side of the church. The niche seen in the wall is typical of the buildings of this period.

Photo 31 The rib-vaulted dome in the south aisle, which Pevsner dates to about 1300, also around the time Robin was active.

Photo 32 The Keep of Conisbrough Castle showing the fine ashlar masonry in white limestone, fully deserving the description 'a fayre castell' included in the Gest. It is also clear from this photograph that the castle was, and still is 'double-ditched about'.

Photo 33 Conisbrough Castle would have obviously have been easily defended. It is not surprising that the Sheriff of Nottingham and his followers gave up their siege after only forty days. Even today, if one avoids using the steps recently provided for the benefit of visitors, climbing the sides of the ditches is very exhausting.

Photo 34 Another general view of the castle.

Photo 35 The remains of the Anglo-Saxon preaching cross or rood in the grounds of Conisbrough Parish Church. The cross is believed to date from about 335AD and is only 260 yards from the castle walls.

Photo 36 Marshes on the north bank of the River Aire close to the site of the Roman ford and a later Roman bridge. Conditions will have deteriorated since Robin's time as a result of recent coal mining subsidence, but on the other hand will have been improved by the construction of subsequent drainage works.

Photo 37 Fairburn Ings Nature Reserve on the north bank of the river created by the flooding of mining subsidence. It is clear that the original ground must have been subject to natural flooding during periods of heavy rainfall making the crossing here very unsafe and unreliable.

Photo 38 The ruins of Saint Mary's Abbey in York where Sir Richard at the Lee went to settle his debt using the funds lent to him by Robin Hood, and from where he returned home rejoicing to Wensleydale (Verysdale).

Photo 39 The River Ure flows through the beautiful and tranquil Wensleydale (Verysdale). It is not surprising that the Gest describes how Sir Richard was rejoicing as he returned here after escaping from the clutches of the Abbot of Saint Mary's.

Photo 40 Winter in Wensleydale.

Photo 41 The River Ure descends over a series of layers of limestone at Aysgarth in Upper Wensleydale less than 20 miles from Sir Richard's probable home at Bedale Castle.

Photo 42 Hardraw Force, England's highest single drop waterfall, is formed by a tributary of the River Ure in Wensleydale. The layers of the different types of rock forming the Yoredale Series are clearly seen.